Jewish Bodylore

STUDIES IN FOLKLORE AND ETHNOLOGY: TRADITIONS, PRACTICES, AND IDENTITIES

Series Editors:
Simon J. Bronner, Pennsylvania State University, Harrisburg,
emeritus and Barbro Klein, Stockholm University, emerita

Advisory Board:
Pertti Anttonen, University of Eastern Finland;   Julia Bishop, University of Sheffield, England; Ian Brodie, Cape Breton University, Nova Scotia, Canada; Lei Cai, Wuhan University, China; Norma Elia Cantú, Trinity University, San Antonio, USA; Valdimar Tr. Hafstein, University of Iceland; Petr Janeček, Charles University, Czechia; Hideyo Konagaya, Waseda University, Japan; Peter Jan Margry, University of Amsterdam, Netherlands; Ulrich Marzolph, Georg-August University, Göttingen, Germany; Thomas A. McKean, University of Aberdeen, Scotland; Rūta Muktupāvela, Latvian Academy of Culture, Riga; M.D. Muthukumaraswamy, National Folklore Support Centre, Chennai, India; Francisco Firmino Sales Neto, Universidade Federal de Campina Grande, Brazil; Anand Prahlad, University of Missouri, USA; Süheyla Saritas, Balikesir University, Turkey; Dani Schrire, The Hebrew University of Jerusalem, Israel; Pravina Shukla, Indiana University, USA; Diane Tye, Memorial University of Newfoundland, Canada; Ülo Valk, University of Tartu, Estonia

Studies in Folklore and Ethnology: Traditions, Practices, and Identities features projects that examine cultural traditions around the world and the persons and communities who enact them. Including monographs and edited collections, the series emphasizes studies of living folk practices, artists, and groups toward a broad understanding of the dynamics of tradition and identity in the modern world.

Recent Titles

Jewish Bodylore

Feminist and Queer Ethnographies of Folk Practices

Amy K. Milligan

LEXINGTON BOOKS
Lanham • Boulder • New York • London

Published by Lexington Books
An imprint of The Rowman & Littlefield Publishing Group, Inc.
4501 Forbes Boulevard, Suite 200, Lanham, Maryland 20706
www.rowman.com

6 Tinworth Street, London SE11 5AL

British Library Cataloguing in Publication Information Available

Library of Congress Cataloging-in-Publication Data

Names: Milligan, Amy K., 1982- author.
Title: Jewish bodylore : feminist and queer ethnographies of folk practices / Amy K. Milligan.
Description: Lanham, MD : Lexington Books, [2019] | Series: Studies in folklore and ethnology: traditions, practices, and identities | Includes bibliographical references and index.
Identifiers: LCCN 2018052568 (print) | LCCN 2018055015 (ebook) | ISBN 9781498595803 (Electronic) | ISBN 9781498595797 (cloth) ISBN 9781498595810 (pbk.)
Subjects: LCSH: Human body—Symbolic aspects. | Symbolism in folklore. | Human body—Religious aspects—Judaism.
Classification: LCC GT495 (ebook) | LCC GT495 .M55 2019 (print) | DDC 306.4—dc23
LC record available at https://lccn.loc.gov/2018052568

For Dan Milligan, z"l
I will always love you more.

Contents

Acknowledgments

As a child, my favorite school programming was "Writing Workshop." After working on drafts of our stories, we had the opportunity to meet with an "editor" for feedback on how to improve our writing. Finally, at the culmination of our writing project, we could publish our book. A dutiful parent volunteer would peck out our story on a typewriter, leaving enough room at the top of the page for us to illustrate the text. After the illustrations were created, the pages were bound using cardboard and brightly colored tape, creating a book that was housed in our classroom library. At one point in second grade, Miss Greenfield, my cherished teacher, had to tell me that I couldn't publish any more books for our library because other children needed a chance to work with the volunteers. I was devastated. Anticipating this response, Miss Greenfield had a plan: I could begin writing chapter books. She promised that if I worked diligently on an arch of thematic content that I could publish the *ultimate* chapter book instead of a series of smaller books. Thrilled by this prospect, I began a "comprehensive" story about a little girl who loved reading and dogs. Nearly three decades later as I began writing this manuscript, I paused to reflect—I guess some things never really do change. Both that first "chapter book" and this current text were written by a girl who loves books and dogs, although I didn't have anyone volunteering to type out pages for me this time! But this book would not be possible without the constant support of many who have helped it come to fruition.

This book is dedicated to my father, Dan Milligan (z"l). He always said, "you got your brains from your mother," but if that is true, I hope that I got my heart from him. He not only underestimated his own intellect, but he also did not credit himself for his empathy and kindness. A proud soldier who worked a blue-collar job his whole life, he put up a gruff exterior. Underneath that facade was a man who drove out of his way after work to walk the dog of an elderly woman he barely knew so that she wouldn't have to give up her beloved companion; a man who stopped at every lemonade stand run by children and smacked his lips approvingly while drinking their lukewarm concoctions; and a man who bought gift cards at the local grocery store to give to my students who were homeless and hungry. Every day I try to live up to that type of radical compassion and am grateful to have had such a great man as my father.

My husband, Heiner Kessler, is my anchor. He makes me laugh even on my darkest of days, challenges me intellectually, and indulges my deeply held convictions, including adopting senior dogs and rigorous home recycling programs. My mother, Kathy Milligan, is my rock. She is my best friend, the only person I can tolerate talking on the phone with for more than ten minutes, and my favorite travel partner. And, as my second-grade self would remind me, my beloved canine family members also deserve recognition: Clara (who, even in her last days, snored through most of my work with absolute disinterest) and Darcy (who faithfully and attentively monitors me at all hours while I write).

Simon J. Bronner will likely point out that he came after the dogs in my acknowledgements. His mentorship has been profound both personally and professionally. This book is a direct result of his encouragement. When I have stalled in the writing process, I remind myself "WWSJBD?" (What Would Simon J. Bronner Do?) and dive back in. He is the man who first told me I was a folklorist, my constant intellectual sounding board, and a cherished friend.

I am indebted to my faculty writing group at Old Dominion University, who helped birth this text or at least kept me caffeinated during its creation, especially Liz Black (and her bike basket), Remica Bingham-Risher, Liz Groeneveld, and Kerstin Steitz. Additionally, I am grateful to Vanessa Ochs, Nazareth College's Hickey Center for Interfaith Studies and Dialogue, and the University of Colorado-Boulder's Jim and Diane Shneer Fellowship in Post-Holocaust American Judaism, who have all provided feedback or support on various parts of this project. I am deeply grateful for the dream team of female clergy who inspire me, feeding both my soul and my intellect: Rabbi Roz Mandelberg, Cantor Jen Rueben, and my lifelong best friend, Rabbi Leah Berkowitz. Additionally, I am thankful for the support of friends and colleagues, including: Jennifer Fish, Terri Hughes, Heather Kanenberg, Lee Ellen Knight, MaryCatherine McDonald, Carly Miller-Carbaugh, Elizabeth Milligan, Juliane Näder, and Cathleen Rhodes.

Introduction

Jews, Gender, and Bodylore

My German mother-in-law, Irmhild, collects angels. Her collection includes angels made of wood, glass, ceramic, ivory, and metals—sculpted, painted, and stylized in every imaginable way. One afternoon, sitting in her living room surrounded by more than a dozen of her angels, I commented aloud, "None of your angels has dark hair." We looked over her collection and it was true: nearly all of her angels had blonde hair and the few outliers had light brown or strawberry blonde hair. After two years of searching for a dark-haired angel, she mailed me the "Amy-Engel." She purchased a small blonde angel and glued black yarn over its painted hair. More than just being a physical likeness to my own dark hair, the black-haired angel was a gift that acknowledged that everyone deserves to see representations of herself, both literal and symbolic, because this type of recognition holds power.

In the end, this figurine looks nothing like me (to be fair, yarn hair on a painted angel is a difficult artistic medium), but it does symbolically make me feel "seen." In the same way, other symbols and engagements of the body create a canvas for individuals to script their identities. By engaging the body in these ways, it serves as both a space of self-representation as well as a source of external communication.

This book explores the body and its symbology as a space for identity communication. In the following chapters, I apply the tools of bodylore to the Jewish body in ways that are in line both with feminist and queer theory. In this introductory chapter, I describe the ways that the Jewish body has historically been treated. I identify the central methodological tenets of bodylore and establish the framework of analysis for the subsequent chapters in order to create a cohesive thread that runs throughout these bodylore investigations. Ultimately, using the tools of folklore and the body, I explore feminist

1

understandings of the role of the body and embodiment for contemporary American Jews.

RHETORICAL NOTES

As a writer, I realize how deeply words matter. Throughout this text I have made several rhetorical choices that bear noting.

First, throughout this book, I use the term "anti-Semitism" to refer to both anti-Semitic (i.e., Jews as a racial group) and anti-Jewish (i.e., Jews as a religious group) actions, stereotypes, and forms of hatred. While the words do have different meanings, I use them in their colloquial sense as synonyms and indicate if there is a difference in use.

Second, I use the acronym LGBTQ (lesbian, gay, bisexual, transgender, and queer). I recognize the limitations of any acronym and acknowledge that the identities represented by LGBTQ are not encompassing of all queer identities and that it does not represent the full spectrum of sexuality and gender identity. I have chosen to use the familiar LGBTQ for ease of readership, but it is not my intention to place limits on LGBTQ identities or exclude any voices.

Third, I also use the term "queer" as a synonym for LGBTQ. This usage is in line with its contemporary use within the LGBTQ community, particularly because it offers a wider umbrella for community identification than the acronym LGBTQ. Like all words, the connotation of the word queer varies by generation, context, and intent. I use it here as a reclaimed, positive, and inclusive descriptor of the LGBTQ community.

Fourth, all Hebrew and Yiddish words have been transliterated into Roman characters for readers. I have followed the common *Sephardic* transliteration style. However, because of the overlap between spoken language and written language, as well as geographic and community distinctions, I have followed the common *Ashkenazic* pronunciation style and transliteration for Yiddish words (e.g., *Shabbat/Shabbos*, *tallit/tallis*, *payot/payos*). When using a direct quote or text from a printed source, I have left the author's original spelling unaltered. As with any transliterated language, there are variations of spelling, which I have standardized in my own writing but also reference variations in the glossary.

Finally, I have made every effort to write without academic or Jewish jargon, as I believe material should be accessible to a range of readers. However, some words simply hold more meaning in their original form (e.g., *Bat Mitzvah*, *yarmulke*, *halakhic*). When a potentially unfamiliar word is introduced to the reader, I have included an in-text gloss of the word at its introduction.

Subsequent uses of the word are italicized, and all of these glosses are compiled, some with additional context, in a glossary to assist the reader.

THE JEWISH BODY

The bodies of Jews discussed in this book cannot be separated from their historical context. Although this study of Jewish bodies centers on corporeal engagement with folklore and articulations of Jewish embodiment in contemporary America, the Jewish body, individually or collectively, has a long history of interpretation and representation. One important manifestation of anti-Semitism, both historically and in contemporary contexts, is in the depiction and treatment of Jewish bodies. Often, even more than criticizing the beliefs or practices of Jews, the body becomes the target of anti-Semitic attack. These treatments of the body are undergirded by years of anti-Jewish stereotypes, which make assumptions not only about the appearance but also the perceived genetic inferiority of Jews.

Although eugenicists and other scientists historically tried to prove the racialization of Jews, as well as substantiate other observable stereotypic characterizations (e.g., the hooked nose) (see Gilman 1986; Langmuir 1990; Laqueur 2006), there is not a quantifiable or legitimate measure of the Jewish body. Understandings of the Jewish body are complicated by the fact that Judaism is an ethno-religious identity (Edelstein 2002; Winland 1993). In other words, some Jews identify their Jewishness based on religious practice and others based on secular cultural or ethnic affiliation (Klepfisz 1989; Rich 1986). Unlike other religious groups, which are typified by a particular belief structure, Jews may identify themselves as secular Jews or even as Jews who practice other religions (see Niculescu 2012). Unfortunately, the ethno-religious classification has also been used to racialize Jews (e.g., in Hitler's creation of the master race) or to exclude Jews (e.g., prohibiting the inclusion of a Jew who has converted to Christianity because she is still considered racially Jewish). The Jewishness that I describe in the following chapters refers to an encompassing non-racialized understanding of who is a Jew: anyone who identifies as a Jew is a Jew. This includes those who have converted to Judaism, Jews of all races and ethnicities, those who do not practice or affiliate with any Jewish organizations, those who identify as secular or atheist, those who are active in Jewish secular culture but not religious practice, as well as those who are religious.

There are a number of significant anti-Semitic stereotypes, including the Jewish ghetto girl, the Jewish banker/money lender, the greedy Jew, the overbearing Jewish mother, the Jewish American Princess, the wandering

Jew, and the evil Jew (Booker 1991; Foxman 2010; Mannes 1999; Prell 1999; Saposnik 1994). While this text will not unpack each of these character archetypes, they are typified through the representations of the anti-Jewish stereotypes that are used to encode Jewish bodies. Moreover, the ways in which Jews understand their bodies is shaped by reactions to these stereotypes.

In order to establish the groundwork for discussing the contemporary folklore of Jewish embodiment, this chapter will consider several stereotypical conceptualizations of the Jewish body: horns, tails, and hooves; smell; male menstruation, effeminacy, and circumcision; flat-footedness, asthmatic temperament, and other signs of physical weakness; racialization and eugenics; hair, beards, *payot*, and head covering; hooked noses; and other stereotypes of the Jewish body.

Horns, Tails, and Hooves

One of the most familiar and long-lasting anti-Semitic stereotypes is that of the horned Jew (Straus 1942). Originating as part of medieval Christian iconography, this is a result of a mistranslation of Exodus 34:35, where Moses is described as having a shining face. Instead of translating *karan* (to send forth beams), the verb was rendered *keren* (a horn) (Propp 1987). Because of this, Moses was often depicted with horns, including in popular images created by Michelangelo and Donatello. As most people of the time could not read the text themselves and relied on images to help interpret the text, this underscored public popular belief that Jews did, indeed, have horns.

Jews are depicted as devilish in Martin Luther in "On the Jews and Their Lies" (1543) and in numerous other anti-Semitic treatises of the time. This depiction is primarily based on John 8:44: "You are from your father the devil, and you choose to do your father's desires. . . ." The text is misinterpreted to indicate that the devil is the father of the Jews. This, in addition to characterizations of Jews as pigs, has created extensive imagery that utilizes hooves and tails to identify Jewish bodies. In combination with horns, it is no wonder that anti-Semitic depictions and treatments of Jews as animals are used to dehumanize Jewish bodies.

Smell

Jews were historically also accused of having a particular smell, often described as similar to the smell of sulfur. This accusation is an outgrowth of the association of Jewish bodies with the devil, as it was believed that the devil had a particular odor. Tied to accusations of blood libel, it was believed that Jews who did not emit this smell had used Christian blood to negate the odor. Although often thought to be an outdated stereotype, it resurfaced again during the early 1900s and was one of the areas of scientific inquiry for Nazi scientists.

Male Menstruation, Effeminacy, Circumcision

Jewish male bodies have historically been treated as suspect. Beginning in the 1300s, there was belief that Jewish men menstruated. Stemming from a misinformed belief that the circumcised penis continued to bleed, hence rendering the phallus female, the belief is also tied to accusations of blood libel, or at least a punishment for spilling the blood of Christians and/or Jesus. Labeled as a separate third sex, "menstruating Jewish men" had to suffer monthly menses as atonement for the death of Christ. This belief in the third sex lasted well into the 1800s and manifests in other areas, including both colloquial slang and psychological studies referring to the clitoris as "the Jew" and calling female masturbation "playing with the Jew" (Beusterien 1999; Boyarin 1997, 210; Katz 1999; Milligan 2013, 75–76; Resnick 2000).

Even after the myth of the Jewish third sex was debunked, there was still a strong association between Jewish men and effeminacy and/or homosexuality. Depicted as soft and feminine regardless of sexual orientation, Jewish men were categorized, including in the propaganda campaigns of Nazi Germany, as weak or womanly. Undergirded by important psychological studies—which have since been discredited—like Otto Weininger's *Geschlecht und Charackter* (Sex and Character, 1932), scientists attempted to prove that Jews are characteristically feminine and equated this perceived softness and cowardliness with the downfall of modern society (ibid., 301–30).

Other discussions or understandings of the Jewish male body are tied to male circumcision. Although there is widespread acceptance of circumcision in contemporary American society, historically it has served as a marginalizing body practice. Equated with castration by the Romans, it was even outlawed, as it was seen as an unnatural offense that ruined the natural inherent beauty of the body (Hodges 2001; Robinson and Robinson 1995; Smallwood 2001). Later, when in the letters of Paul (Galatians 6:15) circumcision was defined as obsolete and unnecessary, it began to serve as the marker of identification between Jews and Christians, further solidifying it as a stigmatizing marker of difference.

Flat-Footedness, Asthmatic Temperaments, and Other Signs of Physical Weakness

Jews, especially Jewish men, have been characterized as genetically and physically weak. These stereotypes are in line with the feminization of the

Jewish male body, both in belief (e.g., menstruating Jewish men) and depiction (e.g., Nazi propaganda). Although women's bodies are generally stereotyped as either dirty and poor (the ghetto girl stereotype) or fat and/or rich (the Jewish American Princess or the Yiddishe Mama), men's bodies are typically characterized in two ways: either in caricatures of scrawny bodies with no muscles, often also paired with glasses or other indicators of bookishness (the *bochur*) or in caricatures of obese, sloppy, slovenly, piggish bodies. Both depictions suggest unfit, undesirable, and inferior bodies.

The stereotypes of the unfit Jewish male body have informed stereotypes of Jewish bodies across gender identities. In particular, the perceived unfitness of the Jewish body served as grounds for trying to keep Jews from serving in the military, noting generalized asthmatic temperament and flat-footedness (Gilman 1991, 38–59). Referred to as "The Jewish Foot," low arches or flat feet were considered to represent sloth and unproductive behavior. Moreover, feet are generally concealed in shoes, which furthered the anti-Semitic belief that some Jews were actually hiding their hooved feet in their shoes. Even after the hoof stereotype dissipated, the belief of genetically inferior feet still plagues Jews (Gilman 1990). As the scientific community came to understand Darwin's theory of evolution, the flat foot was attributed to both the Black community and the Jewish community and subsequently seen as a sign of the "primitivism" or lack of evolution for both groups (Ehrlich 1962).

One reaction to the stereotypes of the weak *bochur* (a *Yeshiva* student or bookish Jewish male) was the contemporary Jewish portrayal of the "New Jew." This characterization depicts a tan, muscular, and robust Jewish young man or woman who is working to build the Land of Israel. Iconic in Zionist imagery, the New Jew represents the antithesis of the stereotyped Jewish *bochur* or ghetto girl body (see Klug 2003).

Racialization and Eugenics

As understandings of evolution and genetics increased, so too did racial anti-Semitism, which classifies and targets Jews as a separate racial and ethnic group. Racial anti-Semitism characterizes Jews as possessing genetic traits that are inferior to white Christian (i.e., Aryan) society. Although religious anti-Semites allow for the conversion of Jews, racial anti-Semites believe that a Jew can never shed her Jewishness because it is genetic (Reisigl and Wodak 2005).[1]

Racialized anti-Semitism is especially concerned with the "racial passing" of many Jews. In other words, although not all Jews are white, many identify as white (although by racial anti-Semite standards they are not) (Brodkin 1998; Harrison-Kahan 2005). If a Jew "appears" white, she can "corrupt"

Aryan gene lines in deceptive and malicious ways. Playing off of other stereotypes of sneaky Jews, this anti-Semitic belief not only is concerned with genetic infiltration but also the potential of Jews not being recognized as Jews and secretly "controlling" industry, education, media, or holding other forms of power. The anti-Semitic racialization of Jewish bodies generally does not account for any other racial or ethnic identity, thereby erasing the different experiences of *Ashkenazic* (Jews with German and Eastern European roots) and *Sephardic* Jews (those with Spanish and north-African roots), as well as mistakenly assuming that all Jews identify as or are white (Ferber 1999; Goldstein 2006; Jacobson 1999).

By racializing Jews in this way, eugenics programs (including the Holocaust) have targeted Jews. Similarly, historic laws prohibited Jews from marrying non-Jews, and other forms of anti-Semitic legislation have barred Jews from jobs, civic groups, clubs, fraternities, and institutions of education.

Hair, Beards, *Payot*, and Head Covering

Caricatures of Jews often highlight the hair. These representations depict Jews with dark brown or black hair that is curly or frizzy. These images are often coupled with other markers of Orthodoxy, including beards, *payot*, and head covering. Most commonly the *yarmulke* (a skullcap) is depicted, although some representations of Jewish women also include tattered wigs or other methods of hair covering. The *shtreimel* (a fur hat worn by Hasidic men), usually also paired with a *caftan* (a robe or tonic worn over the clothes) and knee socks, is also used as a marker of Jewishness in images. In all of these cases, hair and its stylization depicts an externalized outgrowth of Jewishness, one that cannot be tamed or denied.

Hooked Noses

The most familiar of Jewish body stereotypes is the hooked nose. Like hair, the nose can also be exaggerated in images and is used as a way of communicating otherness. These images often feature Jews with noses that have a convex nasal bridge, often with a hook or inward tilt of the point of the nose. Studies have shown that this type of nose is not unique to Jews and is equally common in other areas of the world (Helmreich 1982, 36–37; Silbiger 2000, 13). Still, the hooked nose remains the most repeated and recognizable form of Jewish body caricature.

Historically, medical and scientific literature labeled this type of nose "the Jewish nose" and classified it as a deformity or sign of genetic inferiority (Gilman 1991, 169–93; Holden 1950, 69). Sometimes termed "hawk-like," nineteenth-century descriptions of Jewish noses labeled them as "large, massive, club-shaped, [and] hooked" (Kroha 2014, 284; Preminger 2001), and by 1906 Jewish folklorist Joseph Jacobs describes that the Jewish nose can be drawn by drawing the number 6 and by removing section where the final twist meets the original line (1886; 1906).[2]

Stereotyped depictions of the Jewish nose are prominent in anti-Jewish propaganda and political cartoons. The exaggerated nose is often the first way of identifying the Jewishness of the character; this type of anti-Jewish depiction treats the Jewish nose as a joke or a facial-cranial trait indicating inferiority.

With the advent of plastic surgery, the Jewish nose became a pathological archetype that could be corrected, even creating rites of passage for young Jewish women who were given nose jobs for their sweet sixteen birthday gifts. Although pressure remains particularly focused on Jewish women conforming their noses to standards of white western beauty ideals, some Jewish women, like Barbra Streisand, are iconic for embracing their noses as a "signature feature" (Gilman 1994, 364; Reznik 2010; Schrank 2007).

Other Stereotypes of the Jewish Body

In addition to the previously listed stereotypes of the Jewish body, there are several other typecasts worth mentioning. Jews have been characterized as having: shifty, beady, dark, and/or close-set eyes with droopy eyelids; as having rat's teeth or rat's smiles with thin lips or, conversely, over-pronounced fat lips; rounded knees, large ears, low brows, long fingers, clammy hands, or a "repulsive" appearance from behind; fatness (when associated with piggishness or greed) or thinness (when associated with meekness or genetic inferiority); and, among other things, short stature and/or short limbs (Konner 2009).

In addition to the Jewish body's depiction in film, art, cartoons, and propaganda, some performers have also performed in "Jewface." This practice was popular during the 1880s when Eastern European Jews first began arriving in the United States. Like Blackface, Jewface is an offensive vaudevillian performance of Jewish stereotypes. Performers wore exaggerated noses made of putty, long beards, "ghetto" clothing (tattered, torn, worn out), and spoke with affected accents that mimicked the Yiddish accents of Jewish immigrants (Merwin 2007). Although this practice is now considered anti-Semitic, the type of performance finds a softer manifestation in some Jewish comedy and depictions of Jewish characters in film and television. The pale, nerdy Jew, the fat overbearing Jewish mother, or the Jewish comedian's self-deprecating jokes about his curly hair and big nose all continue to utilize the same stereotypes of the Jewish body that have existed for centuries (Dubrofsky 2013; Johnston 2006; Stratton 2001).

In the end, characterizations and caricatures of the Jewish body indicate "otherness." They were first a way of classifying and segregating Jews (e.g., into the medieval ghettos or during the Holocaust), but as Jews have integrated into contemporary American society, images of corporeal difference continue to be significant. There has been a shift from understanding Jewishness as a racial category to conceptualizing Jewishness as a cultural, albeit ethnic, category. Still, the understanding that not all Jews are religious inadvertently substantiates false stereotypes of measurable manifestations of a corporeal Jewishness.

INTRODUCING BODYLORE AS A FRAME OF ANALYSIS

Although folklore had long considered the body, especially in studies of material culture, play, and gesture (Chamberlain 1893; Clair and Govenar 1981; Dundes 1964; Prown 1982; Rose 1919; Taylor 1956; Yoder 1972), it was not until the 1980s that bodylore evolved as a distinct folklore methodology. By giving separate attention to the body as a space of study, bodylorists consider not only the ways in which the body expresses identity and culture, but, and perhaps more importantly, how the body is an object itself (Milligan 2018). Katharine Young organized a panel on the folklore of the body at the 1989 American Folklore Society meeting, conceptualizing "bodylore" as a methodological home for discussions of the body, embodiment, and externalizations of identity as part of navigating culture. Young defines bodylore as the investigation of "a constellation of corporeal properties in order to illuminate a cluster of theoretical puzzles . . . the panoply of possibilities of the body as a discursive focus discloses the underlying suppositions, concentrations, and insights of bodylore as a discourse. We are not in quest of bodies, a body, or *the* body, but of our holds on the notion of bodiliness, of what we invest in the body and what we get out of it" (Young 1994, 3). Viewed through this lens, the body is its own text that is scripted and nuanced, a space where culture and tradition intersect in their transmission and interpretation (Young 1993, 2011).

Bodylore considers how the body is used in communication, in creating social meaning, in depicting identity, and in engaging in social interactions. Because of this, consideration is given to both the personal and private experience of the body, as well as the public performance of the body, how others understand it, and how bodies interact with space and other bodies. Likewise, attention is given to the body as a personal space, one that the individual cultivates through gesture, identity performance, dress, adornment, and stylization. Some of the ways the body is enacted by the individual are personal (e.g., the decision to get a tattoo) and others are more subconscious (e.g., engaging in uptalk as part of how American women are culturally taught to engage speech patterns) (Milligan 2018). Bodylore explores how the body is both private and public, consciously and subconsciously performative, as well as how the body experiences and processes sensation (see Bronner 1982; Classen 2012; Montagu 1971; Sklar 1994) and carries and transmits various identity markers (see Young 1993).

Learning how to engage corporeal symbols and markers is part of the transmission of bodylore, whereby individuals come to understand their situation in cultural scenes and contexts. Bodylorists engage Erving Goffman's "frame analysis" methodology (1974) and his "performance of self" theory (1959) to bring together studies of the body. By using frame theory in tandem with rhetorical criticism and ethnographic analysis, bodylore scripts the body as the text. This centers the body in the narrative, analyzing both the individual and the society in which she lives, allowing for the body to have both personal and communal meaning. Moreover, bodylore offers a way of considering how the body changes based on perception, as well as how individuals adapt their bodily engagements based on situations, identities, change (e.g., getting older), location, or the perceived audience (see Bronner 2010; Mechling 2008; Milligan 2018; Turner and Turner 1982).

The script of the body also takes on group meaning and identification. Familiar examples of this include cultural cues like the Muslim *hijab* (a head covering worn by some women that covers the head and chest) or the Sikh *dastaar* (a religious turban) that have personal meaning for the individual, group meaning for the collective religious group, and also simultaneously serve as markers of identity for outsiders. For bodylorists, these symbols serve as signifiers for how individuals engage their bodies (e.g., how a Muslim woman feels about wearing the *hijab*), as signs of how a cultural or identity group understands the body (e.g., how the *hijab* is viewed within the American Muslim community), and as a way for outsiders to categorize individuals, even if those categories are not always fully recognized or understood (e.g., how American society views or misunderstands the *hijab*). Also of interest for bodylorists is how marginalized body culture can become appropriated by the dominant culture (e.g. dreadlocks, Polynesian tattoos, or the bindi) in ways that commodify stigmatized bodies by including them into the popular cultural vernacular while still undergirding unequal power dynamics (e.g., the perception of wearing a dental grill as "ghetto" or "ratchet" when done within the Black community but cool or urban-chic when worn by a white celebrity).

Ultimately, bodylorists push back against previous anthropological and sociological studies of the body that focused on exoticism instead of everyday body interactions. This approach does not negate considerations of the exotic but engages the body as a text that can be political at the same time that it is personal, a text that is shaped by the individual while simultaneously policed by culture, and a text that speaks to the changing and evolving standards of personhood, culture, community, and society.

APPROACHING JEWISH FEMINIST BODYLORE

This book brings together a series of chapters that highlight various intersections of gender, sexuality, and the Jewish body, commenting on the ways in which Jews have utilized bodylore to navigate tensions of their lived embodiment. Feminist studies of the body largely deal with, as is discussed in chapter 1, issues of the "second sex," women's health and reproductive choices, gendered violence, and, more recently, the experiences of the transgender community. A feminist bodylore methodology is in line with these goals, in that it continues to center the experiences of the gendered and sexed body. It diverges from traditional feminist theory, though, in its coupling with a theoretical folklore of the body. These two things are not incompatible with each other; rather, they are complementary.

Feminist folklore evolved toward the end of second wave feminism in the 1970s. Folklorists who had been affected by the women's liberation movement of the 1950s and 1960s began to apply their feminism to studies of folklore (see Dorson 1972; Farrer 1975; Paredes and Bauman 1972). Feminists challenged the study of folkloristics, calling for a redefinition of who was being studied (Babcock 1987; Stoeltje 1988), as well as asserting that traditional folklore had centralized and normalized the male experience (Personal Narratives Group 1989, 3–5). Feminist theory acknowledges that there are different experiences of feminism and gender, which play out in the folkloric study of the expressions of these differences. If the fundamental goal of feminist theory is "to provide a perspective that relies on female experience and uses this female experience in the production of knowledge, and to respond to women's political struggles and objectives" (Kousaleos 1999, 21), then feminist folklore analysis offers the tools for unpacking experiential and created culture.

Feminist folklorists exist in an inbetweenness. On the one hand, their feminism suggests that they should critique traditional women's practices: Are these roles, beliefs, or folk practices holding women back? How can a woman be liberated if she still engages in practices that may appear, on the surface at least, to be steeped in patriarchy or traditional understandings of home-based womanhood? On the other hand, if feminists do not assert themselves in folkloric study, are these same women at risk of being misunderstood? Are their roles and community contributions marginalized because of their status as women? The feminist folklorist, in her inbetweenness, both lifts up the voices of these women, while still critiquing systems of social and cultural power. Indeed, in many ways these very expressions of women's folklore are relational to the power structures of the society in which the women exist. Whether it is studies of the female agency in fairy tales (Jorgensen 2008) or explorations of the transmission of community values through Mennonite quilting (Cheek and Piercy 2004), feminist folklore addresses one of the stumbling blocks of feminist theory: it allows for women to make traditional choices without labeling them as anti-woman, patriarchal, or antithetical to feminism. This should not be misconstrued to mean that feminist folklore accepts unequal distributions of power or the subjugation of women. Rather, it accounts for those inequalities directly without diminishing the agency of the women engaged in folk practice.

Much of contemporary feminist folklore has been amalgamated as part of intersectionalism or within queer folklore. As someone interested in both of these areas, I can understand the appeal. However, as important as it is to bring these theoretical frameworks into conversation with one another, it is equally as dangerous to believe that they are one and the same. Feminist folkloristics is not merely an interest in the experiences of women. Rather, in line with feminist theory, feminist folklore is a distinct methodology that centers women's voices and experiences, while at the same time investigates structural inequalities, power and oppression, stereotypes, and the cultural coding of gender. Amy Shuman describes this as "a feminist approach to genre (as one aspect of feminist folkloristics) [that] is concerned with identifying the gendered instabilities in classification systems through which women can negotiate and thereby appropriate traditional forms for their own purpose" (1993, 84). Ultimately, feminist folklore explores how women experience, express, and navigate culture without diminishing traditional women's culture as unsalvageable or quintessential at odds with contemporary feminist thought.

It is important to note that feminist folklorists do not adhere to an ideal of universalized womanhood. Indeed, one of the challenges facing feminist folklorists is to articulate experiences of gender without essentializing women or implying universal experiences of gender. At the same time, feminist folklore must lift up women's genres that have been ignored in other studies, including folklore (Farrer 1975; Hollis, Pershing, and Young 1993; Jordan and Kalcik 1985; Lewis 1974; Radner and Lanser 1987; Stoeltje 1988). While it is true that gender cannot be universalized, performances of gender and group identity, even when enacted privately, create bonds between women and their experiences of culture (see Yocom 1985), which is especially pertinent when considering how experiences of gender overlap with other identities (see Mills 1993)

In looking toward the future of a feminist folklore methodology, Margaret Mills challenges folklorists to identify correlations "with other experienced-based critical modes to address the issue of multiple identities through cases—communities, populations, and more especially *ideas* of community" (1993, 187). By bringing this idea of community experience together with Elizabeth Grosz's research on the phenomenology of the body and mind (1994), a "corporeal feminism" can be articulated (see Budgeon 2015; Parkins 2000). Although bodylore is not explicitly feminist in its study of embodiment, many bodylorists engage feminist lenses with their work (Jorgensen 2008; Kapchan 1996; Kisliuk 1997; Milligan 2014a; Young 1994). Kousaleos identifies this as a way of "allow[ing] women to speak the body—to discuss and explore how their physical experiences shape the way they form meaning" (1999, 28). Feminist bodylore, then, is a transdisciplinary and transferrable approach to the body that is attuned to the structures governing, created by, and challenged by the body, in addition to the culture surrounding, embodied in, and explored by the body, its expressions, and the meanings it creates.

My work in the following chapters follows in the footsteps of the feminist folklorists and bodylorists who have pushed against traditional patriarchal methodologies and redefined the treatment of women's bodies. In my research, the community lens is on contemporary American Jews and the experiences of the gendered and sexed Jewish body. I write as a member of a Reform Synagogue in the South, a professor of Jewish Studies and Women's Studies, a cisgender white woman in her mid-thirties, and as someone deeply concerned with social justice. I identify myself primarily as a feminist ethnographer, bodylorist, and folklorist, although my work is informed by queer theory and the theoretical frameworks of intersectionality. Even my discussions of LGBTQ culture in the following chapters are framed by my foundational feminist understandings of the body and experiences of embodiment. This is not to negate the importance of queer theory but rather to situate myself in the larger theoretical and methodological conversation around feminism and queerness. I do not see them as fundamentally at odds with each other but rather as complementary frameworks of analysis.

In articulating an expressly feminist approach to bodylore, my goal is to center a feminist folkloric approach to the body while also recognizing its overlaps with the study of Jewish bodies and symbols. This study delves into the intersections of Jewish identity using a hybrid feminist bodylore methodology. It investigates Jewish embodiment with a keen eye to the subversive, that is to say, investigating that which breaks from tradition. Consideration is given to the ways in which bodies intersect with time and space in the synagogue, within religious movements, in secular culture, and in childhood ritual. Representing a unique approach to contemporary Jewish Studies, this study argues that Jewish bodies and the intersections they represent are at the core of understanding the contemporary Jewish experience. Rather than abandoning or dismissing Judaism, many contemporary Jews use their bodies as a subversive canvas, claiming space for themselves, demonstrating a deliberate and calculated navigation of *halakhah* (Jewish law), and engaging a traditionally patriarchal symbol set which, as they use it, amplifies their voices in a context which might otherwise silence them. Through these actions and choices, contemporary Jews demonstrate a nuanced understanding of their public identities as gendered and sexed bodies and a commitment to working toward increased inclusivity within the larger Jewish and secular communities.

There are a multitude of examples from which I could have chosen, but the topics covered in the following chapters were specifically selected to address key elements of the subversiveness of Jewish feminist bodylore. As a researcher, I am particularly interested in the voices on the margins and, in this case, the bodies that inhabit those decentralized roles. I have chosen the examples in the following chapters specifically to represent the religious (chapter 1, synagogue life), the secular (chapter 4, LGBTQ young adults), and home-based innovative ritual (chapter 3, *upsherin*). Likewise, I have chosen voices that are frequently overlooked in other studies, including the Renewal movement (chapter 2) and queer Jews (chapter 5). In the end, my goal was to select examples that articulated an application of Jewish feminist bodylore as a methodology, and which did so by centralizing the voices often excluded from other studies. The discussions and applications of feminist bodylore as a methodology found in these chapters is transferable to other "traditional" examples of the Jewish body, but as a feminist folklorist, I challenge readers to consider the rich ways in which the voices on the margins can help us rearticulate our own preconceived notions of the body. Each of the following examples is a snapshot of one form of corporeal engagement, demonstrating the diverse and multifaceted ways in which Jews have engaged their bodies, brought together in the conclusion of potential future applications of the methodology.

My approach to Jewish feminist bodylore begins with this introduction and continues in chapter 1, "The Subversive Jewish Feminist Body: Engaging Jewish Women's Bodies in Synagogue Life," where I consider the Jewish feminist reclamation of the literal physical body in Jewish communal spaces. I contend that Jewish feminists, existing on the fringes of both secular and religious culture, can articulate their intersecting identities through the literal embodiment of their Jewishness. By engaging a patriarchal symbol set, these women use their bodies as a place of political subversion, regardless of their actual intent. In doing so, they not only claim space for themselves in ritual and religious life, but they also pave the way for the next generation of Jewish women. I further address the intersection of feminist theory and bodylore, framing a hybrid methodological approach to religious body investigations that is sensitive to the needs of feminists. This is followed by querying the role of female identified bodies in synagogue life, discussing the politicized Jewish body and analyzing the corporeal symbol set utilized by some Jewish feminists. Ultimately, I argue that through this engagement of the body, Jewish feminists demonstrate a deliberate and calculated navigation of *halakha* through which they express a nuanced understanding of their public identities and a commitment to working toward increased inclusivity within the larger Jewish community.

This is followed in chapter 2, "Renewing Her Body: The Body as a Feminist Ritual Text in the Jewish Renewal Movement," with an application of the Jewish feminist bodylore framework. In this chapter, I consider the Jewish Renewal movement and how ritual and community innovations have manifested on the bodies of Jewish women. I contend that Jewish Renewal feminists, who are considered to be a counter-cultural group within Judaism, articulate a nuanced understanding of their lives as women in both secular and religious society by engaging a symbol set that had previously been denied to them. In doing so, they reclaim their bodies, claiming space for themselves in ritual and religious life. In this chapter, I introduce the Renewal movement and discuss the ways in which the movement uniquely engages the body (ecstatic worship; voice; movement and dance; drama, yoga, and facilitating craft) utilizing the framework of "redoing Jewishness." Ultimately, I argue that the Renewal movement utilizes the body as a feminist text on which intersecting identities coalesce, bringing the spirit and the body together in feminist and deeply meaningful ways.

I follow this vein of feminist practice in chapter 3, "Rebellious Hair: Jewish Feminist Reinterpretations of the Orthodox Jewish Ritual of *Upsherin*." *Upsherin* is commonly practiced among the most religiously observant Jewish communities, typically among the Hasidic, Haredi, and Orthodox communities. *Upsherin* includes both a haircutting ritual and a school initiation ritual for young Jewish boys. In this chapter, I contextualize contemporary feminist reinterpretations of this practice, offering both an overview of the Orthodox practice, followed by a thick description of one example of a feminist *upsherin*. I situate the practice in Jewish ritual studies and Jewish feminism, offer a contextualized analysis of the ritual, and ultimately argue that feminist *upsherin* is a distinct and innovative feminist ritual and not an iteration or adaptation of the Orthodox *upsherin* for boys. I contend that the ritual reinterpretation for young girls represents a Jewish feminist folkloric engagement of Jewish tradition, creating space for Jewish feminist voices through the literal embodiment of Jewishness. By marking female bodies, the ritual moves beyond the creation of an egalitarian parallel and inverts religious gender norms to ensure the centralization of girls' voices in private Jewish practice, public synagogue life, and Jewish education.

I extend considerations of Jewish feminist bodylore to also include approaches to sexuality and gender identity in chapter 4, "The *Rosa Winkel*: Jewish Navigation of the Reappropriation of a Nazi Symbol by LGBTQ Young Adults." I explore the question of why the pink triangle has gained recent importance and how it is being symbolically reframed by a new generation. I trace the history of the pink triangle and its usage from Hitler's Europe to the formation of the American gay rights movement. Following this, I analyze contemporary usage of the symbol, with particular attention to the tension that exists between perceptions of empowerment versus victimization. Ultimately, I conclude that the pink triangle is a natural folkloric response by young LGBTQ adults who find voice through the symbol by using it to construct a sense of shared community history and values.

This consideration of queer Jewish symbols continues in chapter 5, "Queerly Stitched: Religious Garb and LGBTQ Jewish Pride Symbols." In this chapter, I discuss contemporary discussions of intersectionality, specifically probing the question of why certain symbols take on significant meaning in social scripting when they are expressed on the body. I offer an overview of the history of LGBTQ acceptance in the Jewish community, followed by a detailed description of Jewish LGBTQ body practices and pride symbols. Ultimately I argue that, through the presentation of the self, queer Jewish symbology challenges the privatization of contemporary American culture in ways that shift the understanding of social scripts such that the body becomes the central texts for navigating overlapping Jewish and LGBTQ identities.

Finally, in the conclusion, "Applications of Jewish Feminist Bodylore," I offer a conclusion and final arguments to the text. I discuss four common themes, including how the examples discussed offer a narrative of how the body can be re-embodied, highlight the potential for multiple interpretations of symbols, discuss reconceptualization of the gendered Jewish body, and articulate the importance of creating space on the body for the transmission of culture and community formation. I also offer five potential future applications of Jewish feminist bodylore, including considerations of the transgender community, race, age, digital bodies, and differently abled Jews.

In the end, this book is a foray into the world of Jewish bodies, how they can be conceptualized using folkloristics, and how feminist methodologies of the body can be applied fairly to Jewish bodies. I challenge methodological frameworks that are predicated on anti-Semitism, racism, and patriarchy, and center the unique experiences of Jewish feminist bodies in ways that allow the bodies to script their own narrative rather than adapting or imposing an outside social or cultural script. Jewish feminist bodylore celebrates the multitude of ways in which the body can be conceptualized and experienced.

NOTES

1. Eugenic or racialized considerations of Jews are anti-Semitic. However, as a population that has historically been predominantly endogamous, there are genetic screenings for certain conditions that can benefit the individual or family; for example, screening for Tay-Sachs disease. This can be likened to screenings for multiple sclerosis within the Amish community. These screenings are optional, not used to marginalize the individual, and completed with informed consent as a medical or preventive health measure.

2. Interestingly, Jacobs refers to "nostrility" in his text. The Oxford English Dictionary notes that this word dates to the late nineteenth century, defining it as "prominence of the part of the nose surrounding the nostrils." It would seem likely that the advent of this word ties to the building anti-Semitism of the time.

Chapter One

The Subversive Jewish Feminist Body

Engaging Jewish Women's Bodies in Synagogue Life

My childhood best friend, Leah, is a rabbi; when her parents tell strangers that one of their children is a rabbi, it is regularly assumed that it is one of her two brothers. This case of mistaken identity is a regular occurrence for female rabbis—underscored by the fact that it is even necessary to rhetorically label "rabbi" with the qualifier "female." The invisibleness of the female rabbi extends into boardrooms, community meetings, and even Jewish spaces. Tired of this phenomenon, Leah created a "This is What a Rabbi Looks Like" T-shirt. After putting the design online, it became a popular gift, especially for newly ordained women (Berkowitz 2009). Now women wear the shirts in synagogues, as well as at Planned Parenthood marches, Black Lives Matter protests, community events, and as street wear. A positive reminder of the fact that women are in the rabbinate, and especially that young women hold this central position in Jewish life, the T-shirt represents one way of reclaiming the Jewish female body, painting it as a political canvas for Jewish identity.

In this chapter, I consider the Jewish feminist reclamation of the literal physical body in Jewish synagogue life. This text understands the feminine or female body to be inclusive of all those who identify as woman, placing no limits on identity or willingly engaging in exclusionary body politics or practices. I use the term feminist to refer to women who identify ideologically with feminism, as well as to label actions taken by women that are a reclamation or empowerment of the feminine, regardless of whether or not these actions are labeled as feminist. I contend that Jewish feminists, existing on the fringes of both secular and religious culture, can articulate their intersecting identities through the literal embodiment of their Jewishness. By engaging a patriarchal symbol set, these women use their bodies as a place

19

of political subversion. In doing so, they not only claim space for themselves in ritual and religious life, but they also pave the way for the next generation of Jewish women. In this chapter, I address the intersection of feminist theory and bodylore, further articulating a hybrid methodological approach to religious body investigations. I query the role of female identified bodies in synagogue life, discussing the politicized Jewish body and analyzing the corporeal symbol set utilized by some Jewish feminists. Ultimately, I argue that through this engagement of the body, Jewish feminists demonstrate a deliberate and calculated navigation of *halakha* through which they express a nuanced understanding of their public identities and a commitment to working toward increased inclusivity within the larger Jewish community.

METHODOLOGICAL INTERSECTIONS: FEMINIST THEORY AND BODYLORE

Feminist theory is familiar with the body as a contested space (Price and Shildrick 2017). Historically, the idea of fundamental biological gendered differences has been used to dismiss or degrade the feminine. Early feminists utilized these arguments of the gendered body housing a non-gendered mind to articulate their equality of thought (Mill and Taylor Mill 1970; Wollstonecraft 1996), unintentionally further enforcing biological determinism. This belief was not universal, as can be seen in Sojourner Truth's assertion that her body could be as strong as any man (Truth 1851) and Elizabeth Cady Stanton's equation of the marginalization of black and female bodies (Stanton, Anthony, and Gage 1887, 680–83). However, these ideas of entrenched corporeality reinforced the idea of women being hardwired for motherhood, while also undergirding the belief that women are emotionally and physically weaker. Viewed through this lens, the female body functions in a double bind: it is both fundamentally corporeal and trapped by this inherent weakness (see Weiss 2013; Witz 2000).

Contemporary feminist theorists have attended to the physical body, largely in terms of conversations about the "second sex," trans body politics, women's health, violence against women's bodies, and the powers of the biologically female (reproductive) body (Bartky 1990; Bleir 1984; Bornstein 1994; De Beauvoir, 1953; Firestone 1970; Martin 1987; O'Brien 1981; Rich 1979; Ruddick, 1989; Young 2005). These discussions of the female body establish a theoretical framework crucial for explorations of female embodiment across disciplines (see also Birke 2000; Davis 1997; Diprose 1994; Gatens 1996; Grosz 1994; Leighton 2012; Weiss 2013). This chapter utilizes the foundational centering of the female body and destabilization of gender found in these feminist body discussions and couples it with the theoretical frame-work of bodylore (Young 1993) in order to probe questions of the female physical body as a space of protest. In contrast to traditional feminist meth-odological body frameworks (which largely address biological determinism, perceived sexed differences, gender performativity, reproduction, and body image), bodylore uses the tools of folklore to probe questions of the body (Hollis, Pershing, and Young, 1993; Leighton 2012; Radler 1993). It evalu-ates gendered performance in tandem with other identity performances and, most importantly, focuses on the situated context of the body, specifically asking questions about the literal corporeal canvas and how the individual has shaped or cultivated that external representation of the self (see Pitts-Taylor 2015). In this case, bodylore does not exist separately from feminist theory, but rather the two inform each other, shaping the study of contentious femi-nist bodies, allowing their feminist statements and their cultural entrenchment to remain intertwined.

Bodylore recasts traditional religious behaviors, which are often dismissed by feminist discourse, considering both the intention of women and the im-pact of their actions on their audience. As a theoretical framework, bodylore highlights the performative aspects of the body. In line with Judith Butler's feminist analysis of the body and its performance of gendered subjectivity (Butler 1990; 1993; 2004), bodylore understands the body to exist within a cultural framework, one which is malleable throughout the daily experiences of an individual. Using its lens of folklore, bodylore adds another layer to Butler's performative analysis in its consideration of gendered symbol sets (Bronner 2005; Leighton 2012; Milligan 2017). While Butler certainly ex-plores the use of gendered symbols of the body in her work, bodylore meth-odologically enables the symbol set of Judaism to be dismantled in two ways. First, in line with feminist theory and Butler, the symbols exist within the gendered performative framework. For example, *yarmulkes* (the traditionally male skullcaps worn by Jews, also known as *kippot* in Hebrew) are encoded culturally with maleness; women can problematize the symbol by wearing it. Second, and this is where bodylore diverges from feminist theory, bodylore accounts for the continuance of symbols within religious tradition while, at the same time, situating it in a gendered and cultural context. Many feminist approaches to religion eliminate, replace, or render patriarchal religious sym-bols egalitarian; in contrast, bodylore centralizes the narratives of women who use patriarchal symbols, allowing feminists to reform from within the masculine structures they inherited by utilizing their bodies as they dismantle the larger system. While this acceptance of the traditional or the religious may seem initially at odds with feminist thought, it represents a progressive un-derstanding of how the bodies of women become the literal intersecting point of contemporary identity politics. Moreover, in contrast to feminist theory, bodylore uses the tools of folklore to probe questions of material culture and the significance of the physical object. If we inhabit our physical bodies, we do so wholly as individuals with multifaceted and complicated identities; the folklore of our bodies is an outgrowth of the sometimes-incongruous identities that we embody.

JEWISH FEMALE BODIES INHABITING TIME AND SPACE

Historically, consideration of the Jewish body has focused on men. This attention has not always been positive; indeed, for many years Jewish men were believed to menstruate and were treated as a third sex (Boyarin 1997, 210; Milligan 2013, 75–76), and as such were homoerotisized and described as soft or feminine. Otto Weininger's *Geschlecht und Charakter* (Sex and Character, 1932) uses physiological and scientific methods in an attempt to prove that Jewish men lack the strength and fortitude of Christian men, and therefore are cowardly, effeminate, and ultimately the pitfall of modern society. Whether it be the Third Reich's oppression or Sander Gilman's research on the stereotypical asthmatic, flat-footed, "inherently unfit" Jewish male body (1991), the bodies of Jewish men have faced significant misrepresentation and violence.

In contrast, within studies of Judaism, the male body is centralized. Although relatively few investigations specifically consider Jewish male bodylore (see Baizerman 1992; Blau 2003; Davis and Davis 1983; Mark 2003; Milligan 2017; Pinson, 2010; Sztokman 2011), the male body is central in synagogue and religious life. In discussions of ritual life, the presence and involvement of men is assumed. Much like it is necessary to specify "female rabbi" when speaking of a woman in the rabbinate, it is also necessary to specify "egalitarian *minyan*" (the quorum of ten required for certain religious events or rituals, traditionally ten men) or "woman wearing a *yarmulke*," because, unless otherwise specified, the male body is the normalized default.

The literal body of the Jewish woman, in contrast, has been under-theorized, particularly in liberal Judaism. Attention has been given to the role of hair and hair covering, as well as variations of the traditional or folk dress of Orthodox Jewish women (see Bronner 1993; Carrell 1999; Milligan 2014a; Schreiber 2006); however, little has been written which theorizes the female body in Reform, Reconstructionist, Renewal, and Conservative Jewish spaces (see Darwin 2017; Milligan 2014b; Silverman 2012). With the majority of Jewish women in the United States identifying as non-Orthodox, why have their literal physical bodies been peripheralized?

First, it is prudent to note that, outside of bodylore, physical bodies and their folkloric symbolic inventories are largely under-theorized. This lack of attention is compounded by any form of "minority" designation; therefore, the bodies of Jewish men are less theorized than the bodies of Christian men, and, as an extension, the bodies of Jewish women are less theorized than those of Jewish men. The disparities are even more pronounced when factors like race, ability, gender identity, and sexuality are taken into account.

Second, the bodies of Jewish women are under-theorized in Jewish spaces because they exist on the margins of worship. Traditional Jewish spiritual life, particularly in the synagogue or in public religious ritual, is male-centric. The role of women within Jewish public practice has experienced substantial evolution, although these gains remain contentious. It was not until 1845 that rabbis at the Frankfort Synod agreed to count women toward a *minyan* in Reform synagogues; it would not be until 1973 that Conservative Judaism would recognize women's bodies as included in *minyanim*, adding the caveat that non-egalitarian *minyanim* are not viewed as breaking Jewish law and are therefore still a viable choice within the Conservative movement (Fine 2002). Similarly, Sally Preisand was ordained in 1972 as the first female rabbi in the United States,[1] followed by the Conservative ordination of Amy Eilberg in 1985 (Greenberg 1988; Grossman and Haut 1992; Nadell 1998; Ner-David 2000). In 2010, the first female Orthodox rabbi, Sara Hurwitz, was ordained, although her ordination remains contested within Orthodoxy. Using the title "Rabba" to distinguish herself as a female rabbi, she formed Yeshivat Maharat, the only institution in the United States that will ordain female Orthodox clergy.[2]

In Jewish liturgical life, the *cantor* (a Jewish clergy person trained and ordained to lead the congregation in prayer; also referred to as the *hazzan*) has an equally important and prominent role in the synagogue. While it is halachically permissible for any Jewish adult to hold this role,[3] non-Orthodox Jews generally confer the position through ordination. Coupled with the traditional belief that *kol isha* (the voices of women) are *ervah* (nakedness or sexually arousing, therefore inappropriate for religious spaces),[4] it is not surprising that it was only in recent decades that women were ordained to this position. Although some women, like Julie Rosewald (1884) and Betty Robbins (1955) led public liturgy, the first female cantor ordained in the Reform movement was Barbara Ostfeld-Horowitz in 1975, followed by the Conservative ordinations of Erica Lipitz and Maria Rosenfeld Barugel in 1987 (Heskes n.d.).

Overall, the discourse around women's bodies in synagogue life has been largely reactionary; responsa address the actions of Jewish women after they have already engaged in the practice or asked the question, focusing on the *halakha* of whether or not it is permissible for women to participate in or lead public religious rituals.[5] Should women be allowed to stand at the *bimah* (the platform area or alter of a synagogue), to hold or chant from the Torah scrolls, to have their bodies count toward *minyanim*, to wear *yarmulke*s or *tallisim* (prayer shawls, also known as *tallitot* in Hebrew), or to lay *tefillin* (leather boxes holding scripture that are bound to the forehead and the left arm)? At the heart of this debate, do women deserve to have the same rights within Judaism that are afforded, without question or dispute, to men? And how are the literal physical bodies of the women—their very presence a political statement, a subversion of religious law—navigating communal religious spaces?

THE POLITICIZED
JEWISH FEMALE BODY IN THE SYNAGOGUE

The symbolic inventory of the synagogue is imbued with maleness. This symbol set includes ritual garb traditionally worn only by men (*tallisim, tefillin, yarmulkes, tzitzit* [the knotted ritual fringes traditionally worn by observant Jewish men, typically attached to a four-cornered garment], and *kittel* [a white linen robe, traditionally a burial shroud, also worn on special occasions and holidays by some *Ashkenazic* Jews]), space (with men at the *bimah* and, in non-egalitarian synagogues, the *mechitza* [a partition separating men and women in worship]), sound (when women are not allowed to chant Torah or, even in egalitarian spaces, where men still comprise the majority of rabbis and cantors), language (with patriarchal liturgical texts or masculine pronouns for God),[6] and visual cues (Torah scrolls, the *shofar* [a rams horn], stained glass biblical scenes, and memorial plaques). In contrast, the symbolic inventory that is explicitly female includes *challah* (A Jewish bread that is braided and eaten on the Sabbath and most Jewish holidays) and *challah* covers, *Shabbat* candlesticks, the *mikveh* (the bath used for ritual immersion), and Orthodox female hair covering. While the male symbols represent active engagement with public Jewish life, the female symbol set is domestic and private, representing homemaking, sexual purity, and modesty.

Erving Goffman's conceptualization of symbolic inventories and social interactions affords helpful tools to unpack the politicization of Jewish feminist bodies in the synagogue (1959). Goffman recognizes identity kits (Goffman 1965) as a set of symbols an individual navigates, noting that when these identity kits are stripped of the individual that she experiences "personal defacement" (Goffman 1961, 21). These items, symbolic of the individual, her identity, and her self-agency, represent the tools needed to navigate the larger cultural world in which she exists (Goffman 1961, 20). An individual's identity kit uses symbolic inventory to engage self-presentation in a way that conforms to social norms, as well as to create personal meaning. In other words, the choices that we make about how we fashion our bodies have meaning to us personally and are read as cultural texts by our "audience." Goffman identifies that, as social actors, individuals react relationally to each other, using preexisting symbols (including "costumes"), and by engaging in a theatrical performance in each of our social interactions, unless we are "backstage" with our private selves (Goffman 1959).

If Goffman's framework is applied to the bodylore of women in the synagogue, two themes emerge. First, as a result of having a limited female symbolic inventory, women have reconceptualized a Jewish male identity kit for their own performance of public Jewishness. While there has been some movement to create uniquely feminine rituals and symbols (see Broner 1999; Ochs 2010), generally Jewish feminists have applied traditionally male symbols to their own religious practices. Second, in doing so, the Jewish male identity kit has become politicized in its use by women, as it represents a shift in relational expectations and performances of gender in a public religious space.

By engaging a masculine symbol set in public religious life, Jewish women demonstrate a dual understanding of *halakhah*. First, their engagement with a particular ritual object or symbol represents their understanding of that object's importance. For example, by laying *tefillin*, a Jewish woman shows a nuanced understanding of the practice, both of the biblical commandment, as well as the rabbinic texts that expound upon how the practice should be enacted. Second, by laying *tefillin*, a woman demonstrates her knowledge that although there is not a *halakhic* provision stating that women must lay *tefillin*, there is also no *halakhic* prohibition stating that women may not do so. The same is true for most other Jewish rituals and symbols: men are told explicitly that, as performers of public Judaism and the positive time-bound *mitzvot* (commandments), they are obligated to engage with these practices, but there is no *halakhic* prohibition barring women from participation.[7]

By engaging these traditionally male identity kits, Jewish women, often unintentionally, politicize these symbols. A Jewish man who wears a *yarmulke* in a synagogue is not viewed as making a political assertion; however, a woman wearing a *yarmulke* makes a statement. Whether or not she views this practice as political is secondary to the fact that others will view her action as a statement. Dvora E. Weisberg articulates this tension, writing:

> I found most frustrating the fact that many people ascribed motives to my wearing *tallit* and *tefillin* without asking me what my intentions actually were. When I daven [pray] in *tallit* and *tefillin*, I am not trying to make a feminist gesture or prove that I can "pray like a man. . . ." It never occurred to me that the need to be reminded of God's presence in regular, concrete ways was limited to men. . . .I realize that wearing *tallit* and *tefillin* is a highly visible action and one that

arouses strong emotions in other people. I know that what I intend to be my personal commitment becomes a public statement every time I enter a synagogue.
While part of me responds to the opportunity to represent a change in women's
patterns of observance, there is also a part that sometimes longs to be an unre-
markable member of the congregation (Weisberg 1992, 283).

In these ways, the woman's body remains a contested political space, one that
she controls but which others will police through their perceptions. Female
engagement with a public Jewish symbol set is one of potential controversy
rather than a reflection of religious autonomy.

THE JEWISH FEMINIST BODY AS TEXT

Sociologists and folklorists identify the physical body as a cultural text that
can be read and interpreted like other artifacts (Leighton 2012). These approaches consider the body, its fashioning, size and location, posturing,
movement, and physical modification all as embodied culture. The performative text of the Jewish female body in the synagogue includes engagement
with voice, garb, physical presence, ritual, and deliberate political subversion.

First, traditional Judaism considers the female voice to be *ervah* (nakedness). As such, women are prohibited in Orthodox circles from singing in the
presence of men, and some non-egalitarian non-Orthodox congregations use
this to reason against female ordination. Therefore, the literal act of singing
or chanting in sacred spaces is an act of religious agency.

Even in egalitarian congregations, there are many non-Orthodox Jews who
have never attended a synagogue with female clergy at the *bimah*.[8] Moreover,
an entirely female voiced liturgy stands in stark contrast to the anticipated
norm. For example, during Purim, the book of Esther (*Megillah* Esther,
commonly shortened to *Megillah*) is read aloud. Rabbinic sources agree that
women are obligated to take part in the reading of the *Megillah* because of
their "role in the miracle," but disagree as to whether women are allowed
to chant the *Megillah* or if they are only to listen.[9] Contemporarily Jewish
feminists have created feminist *Megillah* reading events, often attended only
by women, where the text is chanted exclusively by female voices. Supported
by synagogue Sisterhoods and by organizations like the Jewish Orthodox
Feminist Alliance, these readings center the female voice, affording women
the powerful experience of hearing the story of one of the few named biblical
heroines retold by a collective female voice.[10]

Religious garb also plays an important role in how Jewish women encode
their bodies in the synagogue.[11] These religious items include the wearing of
tallisim, tzitzit, kittel, or *yarmulkes,* and the binding of *teffilin.* In many ways,

these are the most overt examples of women's embodiment in synagogue life. Indeed, they are visual cues to the congregation; the women wearing them are making an intentional choice about how their bodies and their Jewishness will be perceived. Women wearing traditional Jewish garb signal public religious agency. This is especially pertinent when female rabbis and cantors wear these items, demonstrating their rightful authority and presence at the *bimah*. Some religious garb has been feminized in design, with "feminine" color schemes, motifs (often floral), and even styles (for example, lace or open-weave crocheted *yarmulkes*). In feminizing these items, the symbols are rendered more acceptable for women's use. The creation of a separate symbol set is problematic for Jewish feminists, in that it disrupts the universality of symbols for all Jews. This is not an argument against stylization, especially considering that some symbols like *yarmulkes* and *tallisim* are highly stylized by design, but rather an assertion that women should not be assigned explicitly female versions of religious garb.

Regardless of whether or not she wears religious garb, the physical presence of women in the synagogue can be political. As previously discussed, the role of ordained women creates a visual cue to the congregation about religious authority and leadership. Moreover, there are other physical locations or actions that assert the agency of both female clergy and congregants. The removal of *mechitzot* represents the most literal alteration of the physical space. With the *mechitza* gone, the worship space is no longer divided by gender, and women's bodies are able to move into the prime locations of the front and center, rather than being relegated to the sides, back, or balcony.

Physical location at the *bimah* also creates visibility. In addition to female clergy, this presence also includes female congregants being called as an *aliya* (called to the *bimah* to recite a blessing before and after the Torah reading), serving as the *magbiaha* (the lifter of the Torah), or as the *golellet* (the roller of the Torah who replaces the cover after it is read). Similarly, when bodies are gathered in worship or prayer, counting female bodies toward a *minyan* and the inclusion of women as *B'not Kohen* (daughters of a Kohen, a specific designation within Judaism that references [traditionally patrilineal] descent from Aaron) also signals women inhabiting literal space within public Judaism.

Voice, garb, and physical presence coalesce in the struggles experienced by the Women of the Wall (WOW). This Israeli feminist organization fights for the rights of women to pray at the *Kotel* (the Western Wall). They defy the ultra-Orthodox rules imposed at this holy site by chanting Torah aloud (voice); singing traditional melodies and liturgy (voice); wearing religious garments prohibited in the space like *tallisim*, *tefillin*, and *yarmulkes* (garb); and by claiming of space once a month in the women's prayer section (space), where they pray on *Rosh Chodesh* (the start of the new Jewish month).

Despite members of the ultra-Orthodox community blowing shrill whistles to drown out WOW's voices, and while facing violence and arrest, WOW diligently persists in embodying their Jewishness. Sparking legal battles that have reached the Israeli Supreme Court, WOW literally embodies the Jewish feminist subversive spirit of daring to hold space, raise voice, and mark their bodies in claiming Jewish female agency.

WOW's impact has extended significantly beyond Israel. Women from around the world travel to pray with them, and some women bring their daughters to celebrate their *bat mitzvahs*, where the young women are surrounded by the voices and bodies of Jewish feminists at Judaism's holiest site. Those who are unable to travel to Israel bring WOW's message into their own sacred spaces. Solidarity events have been organized worldwide, where women gather on *Rosh Chodesh* to pray together, study Torah, or lobby embassies on behalf of WOW. Other fundraising solidarity events have occurred, where synagogue Sisterhoods raise money to offset WOW's mounting legal costs. Similarly, some young women are choosing to use WOW for their *bat mitzvah* projects, working to organize social justice and action on their behalf within their synagogues.

Israeli artist Yair Emanuel designed and created hand-embroidered Women of the Wall Four Mothers *tallisim* and *yarmulkes*. When worn in Jewish spaces, these ritual items carry the stories and voices of WOW into worship, making a strong political statement of solidarity with Jewish feminists around the world. After fifty women were detained and jailed for wearing this WOW *tallis* at the Kotel, thousands of women around the world purchased these *tallisim* and *yarmulkes* to demonstrate solidarity.

There are numerous other ways in which women creatively embody their Jewishness in religious space. Beyond WOW *tallisim* and *yarmulkes*, other examples include prominent involvement in life cycle events, the creation of rituals for their daughters (the *bat mitzvah*, *pidyon ha-bat*, *simchat bat*, or *upsherin* for girls, for example), Sisterhood *Seders* (celebrations commemorating Passover), or the inclusion of an orange on the *Seder* plate (see Alpert 1998; Elper 2003). Moreover, items like "my mommy is a rabbi" onesies for babies or "real men marry rabbis" T-shirts (also an affirming statement for gay men, too), pink pussy *yarmulkes*, and Jewish feminist jewelry and tattoos, all demonstrate women embodying themselves fully as women, feminists, and Jews.

THE FUTURE OF WOMEN'S BODIES IN SYNAGOGUE LIFE

If there were ever a doubt that the female body remains political, the pink pussy hat marchers protesting the inauguration of President Donald Trump certainly showed that women continue to use their bodies as a space of protest. These hats claimed the symbolic usage of pink and, of course, interpreted the "pussy" as cat ears. Crafted for women by women, the sea of pink pussy hats is an iconic image. Similarly, for Jewish women, the Women of the Wall, their female rabbi wearing a *kittel* on the *bimah*, or their sisters holding the Torah scroll all represent an embodiment of Jewishness akin to the pink pussy hats. Taking symbols that had represented their marginalization, they claim them to create space for their voices.

The hope, of course, is that there will come a day when claiming this space will no longer be necessary, when the normative assumption will be that all Jews inherit the same symbolic inventory and hold the same central role in Jewish worship. Likewise, that a time will come when we no longer specify only female rabbis or cantors but assume that someone with that title could identify as male, female, both, or neither. The contest over bodies in Jewish spaces continues to evolve, and Jewish feminists are beginning to recognize their own problematic assumptions about gender and sexuality in ways bring heteronormativity and cisnormativity to the forefront of discussions of the body. Egalitarian Jewish spaces are not adequate if they continue to marginalize trans and queer Jews. When considering the body as a text, the rhetoric must be inclusive rather than exclusionary, reflective of an encompassing body of all Jews.

At a recent Friday night *Shabbos* service, I looked up at the cantor and realized he was wearing a Women of the Wall *tallis*. At first I thought my eyes were deceiving me—was a male cantor really wearing a WOW *tallis* at the *bimah*? To be honest, I spent the remainder of the service carefully eyeing it from a distance, cursing my own nearsightedness. After *kiddush* (a blessing said over wine during the *Shabbat*, the Jewish Sabbath), I rushed to ask him about it. There he was, a man, wearing a feminist statement unapologetically in front of his congregation—I recognize the privilege his male body has in a public Jewish space, and, yet, it still gave me great hope that all of our children and congregations see both men and women at the *bimah*, unafraid to embody a Judaism that affirms the voices of women as integral to Jewish life.

NOTES

1. Regina Jonas was ordained as the first female rabbi in 1935 in Germany. Although she served a number of roles as chaplain and spiritual advisor, she was never afforded a pulpit. After continuing her work as a chaplain while incarcerated at Theresienstadt, Jonas was deported to Auschwitz, where she was murdered in 1944 (Klapheck 2004).

2. *Maharat* is an acronym for "Morah Hilchatit Ruchanut Toranit," which means "Torah-based, spiritual teacher, according to Jewish law." Some Orthodox female clergy use this as an alternative title to rabbi or rabba.

3. Shulkhan Arukh, Orah Hayyim, 581. Rabbinic texts make it clear that the role is assumed to be held by a man; Isaac of Vienna, for example, writes that a *hazzan* should have a flowing beard.

4. Gemara Berachot 24a; Mishna Brurah 75:17; Shulchan Arukh, Orah Hayyim 75:3.

5. It is worth noting that women's roles in the home are largely uncontested. Women are generally understood to be unobligated to uphold positive time-bound *mitzvot* (commandments) (see Gemara Kiddushin 29b, 34a, 35a; Mishna Kiddushin 29a, Shulchan Arukh 17:2). The three *mitzvot* typically assigned to women include *challot* (bread baking), *nerot* (candle lighting), and *niddah* (sexual purity) (see Milligan 2017).

6. It should be noted that some *Siddurim* (prayer books), most notably the Reform *Mishkan T'filah* (2007), aim to be fully egalitarian, utilizing gender neutral pronouns for God, the names of the biblical matriarchs alongside the patriarchs, and gender inclusive language (example: "children of Israel" instead of "sons of Israel").

7. When considering symbolic engagement, it is important to note two things. First, religious ritual behavior has been amalgamated with compulsive ritual by some psychologists. Rather than a compulsion, the women engaging in these ritualized behaviors exhibit a calculated and deliberate choice. Ritualized behavior, viewed in this light, represents a form of religious agency and a reclamation of voice in a space which might otherwise silence them. Second, religious critics have dismissed feminist engagement with rituals as emotional or symptomatic of a "female" response or "hysterical" impulse to be involved or to have their voices centered. Similarly, other critics have asserted that Jewish feminists are being disrespectful of tradition and of religion writ large, prioritizing their own politics over the needs or desires of the community. These arguments are typical of the adversity even non-religious feminists encounter, where their biology, anatomy, or identity is used to dismiss their agency. By labeling someone as hysterical, emotional, or political—or, as often is the case, with "an agenda"—her voice is further marginalized in the narrative.

8. Liturgical language continues to be a barrier for many Jewish women. Although historically women were unschooled in Hebrew and, therefore, were unable to fully engage in public synagogue life, that has shifted. Now, non-Orthodox Jews tend to have equal access to Hebrew training and exposure through things like bar/bat *mitzvahs* and childhood Hebrew school. However, in order for Jewish women to give literal voice in the synagogue, they must be fluent enough in the liturgical language to lead services or rituals. Most women are adept enough at reading transliteration during services, but this knowledge does not necessarily translate to confidently leading liturgy in Hebrew.

9. Babylonian Talmud Megillah 2b, Megillah 14a; for specifically women's voices Megillah 4a, Mishna Megillat 19b, Gemara Trachtate Arachin 2b–3a, Rashi Acharin 3a, Tosefta Megillah 2:4; Shut Yehaveh Da'at 3:51; Tosafot Tractate Sukkah 38a.

10. For an example of one of these events or to learn more about hosting a feminist *Megillah* reading, see https://www.jofa.org/Project_Esther.

11. Although often taken for granted by contemporary Jews, the change in worship dress code is a result of feminist practice. Non-Orthodox women, in line with their non-Jewish sisters, now wear a variety of clothing, including pants, open toed shoes and sandals, and, in some cases, sleeveless tops and dresses to worship. It is worth noting that women in leadership, especially at the *bimah*, still face policing of their clothing, often being encouraged to dress "professionally" and modestly in order to "represent the congregation" or to have their authority taken seriously.

Chapter Two

Renewing Her Body

The Body as a Feminist Ritual Text in the Jewish Renewal Movement

Despite being a tech-savvy person, I have not been able to give up my paper planner. I understand the transferability and advantages of a digital calendar, but there is something about the tactile nature of paper that keeps me coming back each year. Since I was a graduate student, in the back of my planner I have kept a list of "current projects" and "future projects." Although I get rid of the planner at the end of the year, I hold onto those lists and file them. In 2011, as a doctoral student, I presented for the first time at a major national conference. After the session's Q&A, I added to the "future projects" list a note, "Met Chava Weissler (Lehigh Univ.). She suggested the body has intersections with the Renewal movement. Check it out!" My work at the time had nothing to do with the Renewal movement, nor did I think I was headed in that direction. Yet, Weissler had seen something in my research trajectory that I hadn't yet recognized for myself—the far-reaching impact of corporality within Judaism and the invisibility of the bodies of Jews who exist on religious margins. Recently I emailed her out of the blue, having not seen her since that chance encounter. I had been pouring over her published research, as well as her archived notes and documents at the University of Colorado at Boulder, who generously supported this chapter's research through the Jim and Diane Shneer Fellowship in Post-Holocaust Judaism. Weissler was gracious in hearing from a stranger and encouraged me to continue probing these questions. Truly a research pioneer of Jewish women and folklore, her work continues to inspire me and other feminist scholars. This chapter attempts to unpack that note, written by a doctoral student who had been inspired by Chava Weissler, that, indeed, the body does intersect with the Renewal movement in deeply meaningful—and feminist—ways. In this chapter I begin by introducing the Renewal movement, discuss the ways in which the movement uniquely engages the body, address how this is a redoing of Jewishness, and ultimately argue that the Renewal movement utilizes the body as a feminist text on which overlapping identities coalesce, bringing the spirit and body together in significant and feminist ways.

THE RENEWAL MOVEMENT

Within American Judaism, there are four commonly accepted major movements (also sometimes called branches or denominations): Orthodox, Conservative, Reconstructionist, and Reform. Their differences are often described in terms of levels of observance, a phrase that can feel dismissive for those regularly engaging in religious practice in more liberal communities. The most pronounced division is between Orthodox and non-Orthodox Jews, with differences between progressive Jews stemming primarily from reliance on Hebrew, differences in liturgy, interpretations and applications of *halakha*, and cultural practice (for example, the wearing of *yarmulkes*).

Several other smaller Jewish movements also exist outside of the familiar four mainstream divisions of Judaism. These include groups like Humanistic Judaism (a nontheistic group that emphasizes Jewish identity through culture and history), Neolog Judaism (a Hungarian group similar to American Conservative Judaism), Jewish Science (a parallel to Christian Science movements, which sees God as a penetrating force and places emphasis on affirmative prayer), and Jewish Renewal (see Malkin 2004; Rethelyi 2014; Rothenberg and Vallely 2008; Umansky 2005). Of these groups, the most familiar to American Jews is likely the Renewal movement. The Jewish Renewal movement originated in the 1960s. Originally called *B'nai Or* (Sons of Light), the group now affiliates under ALEPH: Alliance for Jewish Renewal. The movement's central tenets grew out of the work of Rabbi Zalman Schachter-Shalomi (who, himself, was heavily influenced by Rabbi Shlomo Carlebach). Both Schachter-Shalomi (referred to as Reb Zalman within the community) and Carlebach came out of the Chabad movement of Hasidism (Ophir 2014), so it is no surprise that the Renewal movement combines interests in experiential relationships with God, mystical practices, inventive liturgy, with its (non-Orthodox) emphasis on radical egalitarian and inclusive experiences of community. Renewal Judaism especially embraces those who exist on the margins of congregational life, including single Jews, single parents, LGBTQ Jews, women, differently abled Jews, Jews of Color, and others whose voices are not being centered in the larger Jewish conversation (see Groesberg 2008; Magid 2013; Singer 1993).

Central to the Renewal experience is its openness to experiential liturgy, also sometimes referred to as flexible or mystical liturgy. This includes the incorporation of practices like Buddhist meditation, yoga, crafts, dance, and feminist spirituality into traditional Jewish liturgical customs (Huss 2007; Rothenberg 2006a; Weissler 2007). These practices, coupled with other artistic expressions like music, storytelling, dance, visual arts, and crafts serve as an empowering aspect of individual and community spirituality (Weissler 2006, 65).

Sometimes referred to as neo-Hasidism or New Age Judaism, the Renewal movement has a community-based organizational structure. ALEPH's headquarters are in Philadelphia, Pennsylvania, and smaller groups are organized as part of the *havurah* movement. *Havurot* are pairings or groups of like-minded Jews who study or worship together, often serving as an alternative to formal Jewish institutions (Prell 1989). Renewal *havurot* typically form within or, less commonly, separately from synagogues, allowing for great variance of practice between *havurot*. Throughout the Renewal movement, *havurot* are generally considered "post-denominational" and eschew mainstream characterizations of Judaism. Their focus is on a revivalist cultivation of Jewish spirituality, with a keen eye on both personal wellness and the healing of the world.

The Renewal movement has received mixed reception from mainstream Jewish organizations. Initially considered Jewish rebels or "hippies," the movement has defied these dismissive labels and has demonstrated lasting engagement with Jewish practice. Centralizing marginalized Jews, as well as offering a facelift of traditional practices, Renewal Judaism has created space for a new Jewish experience. ALEPH sponsors numerous initiatives, including the Institute for Contemporary Midrash, the Spiritual Eldering Project, an ordination program (although they do not have their own seminary), Elat Chayyim retreat center, C-DEEP (The Center for Devotional, Energy, and Ecstatic Practice), SOULIFT (regional retreats around ecstatic practice), and their yearly Kallah retreat.

Since Reb Zalman's death in 2014, the movement has remained relatively steady, despite shifts in leadership and assimilation of the central ideas and practices of the Renewal movement into mainstream non-Orthodox Judaism. For example, one of the radical early Jewish Renewal tenets was the full acceptance and inclusion of the LGBTQ community. With increased affirmation and support of the LGBTQ community across non-Orthodox denominations, the groups are now increasingly more aligned in their acceptance of queer Jews. Similarly, the Reform movement also incorporates experiences like spiritual chanting, yoga groups, and meditation retreats into religious practice. As such, even those who do not identify with the Renewal movement are still influenced by its practices. With its focus on the literal physical body, ecstatic worship, and ability to embrace a variety of secular, religious, and Jewish practices as part of the spiritual experience, the Renewal movement remains a driving force of experiential worship and religious change within contemporary Judaism.

THE ROLE OF THE BODY IN THE RENEWAL MOVEMENT

One of the unique factors that distinguishes the Renewal movement from other branches of Judaism is the role of the body in religious practice. That is not to say that movement and the body do not have roles in other Jewish denominations, but the way the body is engaged within the Renewal Judaism is markedly different than other Jewish denominations. The unique role of the body can be seen through its use in ecstatic worship, voice, movement and dance, drama, yoga, and facilitating craft.

Ecstatic Worship

There is historic precedent for rhythmic movement during Jewish prayer and worship. Known as *shuckling* (lit. to shake), Orthodox Jews, in particular, are known for their practice of swaying or methodically bowing during prayer. Also sometimes called *davening* (lit. praying), this movement typifies characterizations of Orthodox practice made by community outsiders; this ecstatic spirituality can appear chaotic, as the practitioner appears to be simultaneously entrenched in the movement while also existing spiritually as separated from the body (Ehrlich 2004; Idel 2012; Jacobs 1972). In addition to *shuckling* during prayer, traditional Hasidic practice also includes dancing, clapping, and even turning cartwheels in front of the Torah.

Beyond rhythmic *shuckling*, which is found across Orthodox communities and in limited practice among non-Orthodox communities, ecstatic movement typifies Hasidic worship. Passed on as both oral and enacted tradition, there are stories of the Ba'al Shem Tov (the founder of Hasidic Judaism, a movement within Orthodoxy) trembling with such fervor that pieces of grain nearby were also seen to shake (Ben-Amos 1976). Similarly, stories are told about Rabbi Akiva moving across a room from corner to corner because of his ecstatic bowing and kneeling.[1] The Zohar explains that "When a Jew utters one word of Torah, the light [of the soul] is kindled [such that] he sways to and fro like the flame of a candle,"[2] which is echoed in the Hasidic teaching that *shuckling* is a result of the soul wishing to leave the body to reunite with God (Ehrlich 2004; Frankiel and Greenfield 1997).[3]

Having grown up within the Hasidic community (itself a renewal movement), Reb Zalman was familiar with the Hasidic correlation between prayer and body movement. As his ideas evolved, he merged these embodied practices with a more liberal theology. Bringing together the mysticism and ecstatic embodiment of Hasidic Judaism, Reb Zalman also embraced egalitarian, pacifist, and liberal world views, creating an experiential worship experience that is unique from both Orthodox and other mainstream liberal denominations. Most distinctively, there is significantly more movement. Rather than being confined by pews, worshipers move more freely in the worship space. Hand clapping, dancing, swaying, and other movement is encouraged and common, unlike the more scripted and structured worship of Reform and Conservative synagogues. While other mainline Jewish denominations have a more choreographed worship experience (sitting, standing, and bowing at the same time), the Renewal worship space flows more freely, with the type of ecstatic worship usually only seen within Hasidic communities.

Voice

Explorations of vocalization in Jewish worship are typically found in musicology and investigations of Jewish singing (Cohen 1950; Cohen 2009; Ross 2016; Schleifer 1995). Likewise, generalized studies of the body typically overlook the voice as part of embodiment, as the voice is viewed as internalized; nevertheless, the voice, its use, and the spaces in which it is vocalized reflect performative bodylore (see Rowe 1999; Tedlock 1990).

Within the Renewal movement there are two particular examples of how the voice is uniquely engaged. First is the practice of Psalm recitation: two individuals are paired together; one recites a Psalm from memory while the other closes her eyes; later the individuals switch roles. This practice creates a sensory experience for both participants. The body is engaged in the act of vocalization, as well as, for the partner, the act of listening (see Bendix 2000). For both participants there is a sensory experience in spacial proximity, similar to the one described by Deidre Sklar in her study of the bodies during a Purimspiel (1994). Sklar identifies that the proximity of bodies in worship is as important as the actions that the bodies take, challenging consideration of the role that skin-to-skin contact has in the experience of the body. In the Psalm Recitation, although the two individuals are not necessarily touching each other, the intimacy of the practice aligns with Sklar's identification of the importance of the engagement of the senses in understanding experiences of the body.

A second vocal practice within the Renewal movement, although less common, is the utilization of breath sounds. Reb Zalman advocated using "Yah" (a breath sound) to replace the name of God in prayers. Jewish tradition prohibits saying the name of God; in liturgical readings the *tetragrammaton* (the Hebrew name for God which is not read aloud by Jews) is typically vocalized as either "*Adonai*" (my Lord) or "*HaShem*" (the name). By stepping away from formalized language, the practice of replacing God's name with a breath sound fosters an unexpected experience both for the speaker and for the listener. This practice, again, uses both vocalization and hearing to engage the body in exploring liturgical or religious text (see Pink 2015). In line with breath sounds in meditation (Farrow and Herbert 1982; Rosenberg 2004), the unique vocalization of God's name centers the speaker on the holiness of the word, as well as challenges the anticipated language for the listener. In this case, breath control and vocalization disrupt the paradigm both of heard language and the patterns and melodies of vocalization. By differently engaging the lungs and airflow, breath sounds enact liturgical language in a deeply embodied way.

Movement and Dance

Often dismissed by outsiders as "New Age" or "touchy-feely," part of the Renewal experience is the movement of the bodies through the space, whether in relation to each other (i.e., dancing with someone, clasping hands, swaying as a unit, or engaging in touch), as well as individually inspired movement. Described by some as "Grateful Dead-head-style dancing" (Cohen 2008), Renewal worship offers space for movement beyond traditional *shuckling*. In this case, the *davening* is a spirited and ecstatic embodiment, either along with the music or in personal prayer, in which the individual or group engages in what Reb Zalman calls "davenology," or a "vibrant spiritual experience" (Schachter-Shalomi and Siegel 2012). At its root, this type of *davening* is the same as *shuckling*, but it appears more ecstatic and unbridled.

Separate from ecstatic *davening* is dance, which is used more deliberately as part of the planned liturgical experience. In contrast to *shuckling* or other forms of davenological movement, liturgical dance engages the body in deliberate movement or performance of liturgy or *midrash* (inventive interpretations of Jewish texts). This type of dance is extremely uncommon in other branches of Judaism, but finds voice within the Renewal movement as one way of positively engaging the body in the religious experience. One practitioner describes, "Well, I think that two things are happening. One is that the liturgical dance movement is growing, which is dance as part of liturgy. And also the whole of dance Midrash. Or the Midrash concept is growing and becoming much more acceptable to people and [the] particular area specialty of dance is taking off . . . the energy is building a tremendous amount of momentum" (STI Video Transcripts 1997).

Dance is not foreign to Jews, although it is not enacted in the same way that it is in other religions. Within Orthodoxy, dance finds a place in ecstatic movement, particularly when dancing to a *niggun* (wordless melody). These dances often take place in circles, where dancers can sometimes dance for an hour or more. Within non-Orthodox communities, dance often is typically relegated to weddings (with the traditional *horah*, often while raising the bride and groom on chairs) or, less commonly, having women dance to Miriam's Song during Passover (see Feldman 1994; Polen 1992; Walton 2011). Israeli folk dancing entered the American Jewish communities in the early twentieth century and quickly spread as a way to connect to Jewish identity, especially to build connections to Israel and Zionism. These dances, characterized by leaping and running, are often performed barefoot and tend to not enter traditional liturgical spaces; rather, they are performed by dance troupes, at Sisterhood events, in youth groups, or at summer camp (Ingber 2011; Reimer 2007; Svigals 1998). Other groups, like New York City's Avodah Dance, use dance as a way of interpreting Jewish texts, ideals, and stories. Avodah describes that they use "dance as a tool for social change . . . [bringing] dance to diverse populations with the goal of uplifting individuals and building community (Avodah Dance, n.d.)."[4]

In the same vein as liturgical dance in Christian practice (Blackstock 2008), dance is used in the Renewal movement as a way of engaging both the audience and the dancer. It pushes against preconceived notions of liturgy and suggests new entry points for both the interpretation of text as well as the perception of text. Although scripted in its choreography, it creates a space for a different way of engaging Jewishness, acknowledging that traditional textual (i.e., verbal) interpretation does not hold universal appeal and that dance is a form of both expression and elucidation.

Drama

Performance as part of liturgy is not limited to just dance (McCall 2007) and extends to incorporate other performance arts like dramatic interpretation. The Institute of Contemporary Midrash, which is affiliated with the Renewal movement, has developed a form of liturgical performance they call "Bibliodrama." They describe this as a way of using "improvisational role-playing with untrained participants to create dynamic contemporary midrash . . . inviting participants to imagine the motivations and relationships, struggles and dreams of our ancestral family" (Institute for Contemporary Midrash, n.d.).[5]

Through storytelling and reenactment, texts and textual interpretation come alive. This process demonstrates the interesting blend of Renewal Judaism, bringing together a strong tie to the past and to traditional interpretation methods (in this case, *midrashim*) with an eye to the future and innovative experiences of text, learning, and worship. Now marketed as a study tool to both Jewish and Christian organizations, the Bibliodrama curriculum has gone online and can be learned by educators across Jewish movements and even other religions.

Yoga

Yoga represents the type of cross-religious engagement that is a hallmark of Renewal Judaism. Unafraid to incorporate other religious practices Jewishly, whether it be liturgical dance or drama, the Renewal movement has embraced various engagements of mind-body practices. Although yoga as a spiritual practice (in contrast to yoga as a commodified or healthy living practice) (Antony 2014) has caused the Renewal movement to sometimes be labeled as syncretistic and not faithful to the goals of true yoga practice or to Judaism, the adaptation of yoga as a Jewish spiritual practice has found foothold within the movement (Charmé 2014; Rothenberg 2006a, 2006b). Those who support the incorporation of spiritual yoga note that Judaism has evolved as a diasporic religion, incorporating various elements and ideas as the diaspora has spread and moved, which certainly does not limit Judaism from continuing to incorporate new practices in contemporary times (Bloomfield 2004; Rothenberg 2006a; Ruah-Midbar 2012).

The Renewal movement was doing yoga years before it became a more widespread practice in the United States. This Jewish interest in yoga was, in part, undergirded by Rabbi Aryeh Kaplan's *Jewish Meditation* guidebook (1985). Kaplan's work appealed to those interested in *kabbalah* (a school of mystical thought) and included meditations on the Hebrew letters of God's name, as well as suggestions for physical movements and gestures during prayer.

Yoga and embodied meditation practices were so important within the Renewal movement that, in 1992, ALEPH established a Jewish retreat center, Elat Chayyim, in the Catskill Mountains of New York. Initially hosting weekly summer retreats in addition to special fall and winter retreats, the center offered classes (including "Jewish-Hindu encounters"), vegetarian food, meditation and yoga instruction, and what they called "a unique prayer experience" which "encouraged intellectual and spiritual exploration and offered an amazing array of Jewish spiritual study (Hazon, n.d.)."[6] The retreat center eventually was sold and became part of the Isabella Freedman Jewish Retreat Center, but it remains affiliated with the Renewal movement and continues to focus on "engag[ing] body, heart, and soul through transformative experiences within a diverse community" as well as model "a variety of unique events, each with its own particular flavor of spiritual practice" as part of "renewing Jewish spiritual practices for sustainable futures" (ibid.).

Craft

Finally, the Renewal movement utilizes craft as a form of physical engagement within spiritual practice. Chava Weissler identifies the "role of the arts [as important] in fostering Jewish spirituality" (Weissler 2010, 31) and broadens her definition of art to specifically include handmade crafts. By not limiting artistic expression to dance, music, and fine art, craft encompasses projects created and never displayed and art created for the home, and, perhaps most importantly, focuses on the creation of the craft rather than the final artistic outcome. Although Weissler's work includes such folk practices as quilt making (whereby the quilter interprets biblical texts and *midrash* through her quilt design), she also identifies other forms of craft, largely associated with "women's work," including cookbooks, costumes, clothing, needle arts, fabric crafts, and weaving (ibid., 32–33). These crafts are a form of spiritual engagement, as they allow the creator both space to mediate/ reflect while creating (ibid., 33) as well as an outlet for interpreting religion and/or spirituality.

ANALYSIS OF THE ROLE
OF THE BODY IN RENEWAL JUDAISM

After considering the aforementioned practices, it is clear that movement and the body play a different role in worship and personal spirituality within the Renewal movement than other denominations of Judaism. That is not to say that Judaism lacks engagement with the body, but rather that Renewal embodiment practices differ from other branches of Judaism. Why is this type of embodied spirituality significant? Does the Renewal movement engage the body in a feminist way and, if so, how is the body imagined differently in these spaces in ways that broaden the understanding of the body to include differently abled bodies? In the end, how does the folklore of the Jewish Renewal body meet the needs of practitioners through engaging the body?

Most studies of feminist religion address how women's bodies are treated by others, specifically things like women's access to worship space, the degradation of women's bodies, patriarchal "ownership" or control over women's bodies, women's reproductive issues, or the role of the "marked" female body (Plaskow and Christ 1989; Ruther 1998). While these questions are of fundamental importance in terms of discussing both egalitarian and uniquely feminist religious and spiritual engagement (Ochs 2010), this chapter brings forth the question of how embodied spirituality in Jewish spaces can be a uniquely feminist body practice. This question rests on the legacy of others who have challenged the role of women in Judaism (Heschel 1991; Plaskow 1990; Ruttenberg 2001), but it utilizes bodylore to highlight the uniquely feminist corporality of the Renewal movement.

Contemporary gender scholarship has been heavily shaped by Candace West and Don H. Zimmerman's theory of "doing gender" (1987). In their theoretical framework (which they have subsequently revisited and revised), gender is something taught and enacted rather than innate. This idea has shaped much of contemporary discourse, including consideration of how both theoretical and practiced religion are gendered. Orit Avishai's work (2008) on "doing religion," for example, assesses how contemporary women reconcile their traditional religious practices with contemporary societal gender expectations. Avishai notes that "religious conduct [is] a way of being," as well as a performance of identity in ways that point to the "constructed nature of religiosity" (ibid., 410). Avishai's work navigates a tension created by the overuse of the binary of religion and women: that women must either choose between traditional religion and, in doing so, accept patriarchal oppression or that women can choose to be liberated, which also includes moving away from religion or, at the very least, traditional religiosity. As Avishai and others demonstrate, great empowerment can come from the act of choosing religion, including adhering to traditional religious practices (Bilge 2010; Burke 2012; Milligan 2014a).

Avishai uses West and Zimmerman's theory of "doing gender" to build a helpful framework of "doing religion." She argues that "religion is a mode of conduct and being, a performance of identity—not only a purposeful or strategic action . . . [and] even when viewed as a strategic undertaking, religion may be done in the pursuit of religious goals—in this case, the goal of becoming an authentic religious subject against an image of a secular Other" (Avishai 2008, 413). Unlike doing gender, which is largely an unconscious performance, doing religion is a cognoscente act in which the practitioner enacts religion as a means of achieving experiences of both the self and the spiritual, or, at the very least, these actions are a way of navigating cultural expectations.

Avishai's work in the Orthodox community highlights the nuances of self-actualization, demonstrating that agency is far more complex than an assumption that religiosity or traditional religious choices indicate acceptance of patriarchy; rather, women find creative ways of navigating religion and religious culture in order to meet their personal needs and desires. In Avishai's findings, though, it is clear that some women "do" religion simply out of observance. That is to say, sometimes religiosity or adherence to traditional religion is not motivated by personal spirituality but instead by other modes of being, whether that is familiarity, finding comfort in repetition and tradition, or because of cultural pressures or expectations.

The theoretical frameworks of "doing gender" and "doing religion" have been brought together by a number of scholars (Irby 2014; Nyhagen and Halsaa 2016; Rao 2015), as well as Helana Darwin in her exploration of redoing gendered religion, which challenges the cisnormativity of these other frameworks and focuses on "how female subjects challenge patriarchal religions to become more inclusive of women by appropriating historically masculinized practices and how such practitioners modify the meanings of these practices to better reflect their gender" (Darwin 2018, 353). Darwin's research, which looks at how women utilize *kippot* in their religious and secular lives, suggests that women can "do gendered Judaism" and, as such, they work to make "Judaism more inclusive for future women [by holding] themselves more accountable to this egalitarian shift—and to other Jewish women—than [to] the patriarchal Jewish tradition" (ibid., 358). The women in her cross-denominational study emphasize that they do not want to change Judaism but rather "redo" it by "expanding the ritual options that are available to women while preserving traditional values" (ibid.). Darwin posits that when the women in her study "do Judaism" (in this case, by taking on practices that historically had excluded them), they are misread by outsiders (even within the Jewish community) as "doing egalitarianism" or "doing religious feminism" instead of "simply doing Jewish" (ibid., 363).

These frameworks, particularly Darwin's "redoing gendered religion," are helpful when considering the role of women's bodies in the Renewal movement. One of the difficulties expressed in women across studies (Darwin 2018; Milligan 2014b) is that their religious engagement or actions are viewed as subversive or political, when, in fact, they engage in traditionally male practices because they find them affirming of their own spirituality. How does this question shift, though, when it is broadened beyond garb to include the literal physical bodies of women?

This type of embodiment is significant in several ways. First, it pushes back against the idea of "doing gender" or "doing religion," as it demonstrates that, at least for many women in the Renewal movement, there is deep spiritual connection to their bodies. They are not engaging in traditional practices like *shuckling*, wearing religious garb, or engaging in ecstatic worship because they are "doing religion," but rather because it is a deeply rooted way in which they encounter their bodies in the spiritual space. Furthermore, they are not "doing gendered religion" in the Renewal space. Although their actions might be viewed as subversive in other contexts, in the Renewal cultural scene, women do not need to "claim" these actions, because the practices are already explicitly egalitarian within the community. They are, in essence, just "doing Jewish." At its core, Jewish Renewal is doing what Darwin labels "redoing gendered religion" by completely reconceptualizing Jewish spiritual engagement. At first glance this may seem antithetical for contemporary feminists, as the movement utilizes many traditional practices that can, to an unfamiliar eye, appear to be rooted in patriarchy. However, the "redoing" of these practices has created a radically inclusive space that honors various types of religious engagement. But is the use of the body in the Renewal movement a feminist act and, if it is, how is the feminist text of the body imagined differently in Renewal spaces?

The use of the body in Renewal spaces is feminist in three specific ways: in its centering of the female body, in its use of space, and in its celebration of different bodies. Feminism, in this case, is understood to be more than just the idea that men and women are equal; rather, feminism works to address intersections of identities and the dismantling of structures of power, demonstrating that all humans deserve equality, equity, and accessibility, and that the mythical norms of sameness and equal access need to be dismantled in order to achieve radical equality. In other words, everyone deserves fair treatment and access to resources but that access may look different based on the needs of the individual.

Within the Renewal movement, there is a historical precedence for the centering of female and queer voices. Emerging at a time when mainstream Jewish denominations were still struggling to incorporate women and the LGBTQ community into their congregations, the Renewal movement celebrated the diversity of gender, gender identity, and sexuality. Reb Zalman's rainbow *tallit* is an iconic representation of this radical inclusion. Designed after he had a revelation during meditation, wherein God created the world by wrapping Gods-self in a robe of shining light. The colors of the rainbow *tallit* have been associated with Kabbalistic ideas (ten divine energies of the Godhead which created the world), but the symbolism of the rainbow translates beyond *kabbalah*, sending a welcoming message of LGBTQ acceptance.

The reimagination of Judaism that the Renewal movement accomplishes is quintessentially feminist. It highlights the feminine side (or potential for an entirely female) God, it explores *midrashim* and reinterprets other Jewish texts to create a textual narrative and tradition for women, and it places women in leadership roles, allowing them to use their voices throughout the movement. Often called neo-Hasidic, the Renewal movement offers women a way of redoing Orthodoxy. In other words, if the rituals and stylization of Orthodoxy appeal to them but are not in line with their egalitarian or feminist values, Renewal Judaism affords women an entry point into this form of Jewish practice. They do not need to eschew Orthodox practices as antithetical to feminism; rather, they can fully engage these practices while still retaining their feminism.

Renewal Judaism's use of space is also feminist. By referring universally to each other as Reb, there is a great equalization of practitioner and clergy, wherein both are utilizing the same title. Furthermore, the worship space is reconceptualized. Although the existing structures of the room limits the freedom of space, prayer often happens in a circle. By de-elevating the *bimah* and placing everyone on the same level, and by removing the "stage" aspect of worship by placing everyone in a circle, there is an equalization of practice. The shift away from a stage-centered orientation is similar to the traditional Eastern European orientation of having the *bimah* in the center of the synagogue. By focusing the attention to the center of the circle or to a point on the circle, the power structure of the worship space is altered, highlighting the equality of all those in the space, and shifting the focus away from a "performance based" liturgy, wherein the rabbi or cantor is directing the congregation. Especially because of the use of dance, *shuckling*, and other ecstatic movements during worship, the *bimah*-shift is essential in experiencing the space in feminist and embodied ways.

Furthermore, the space is also used differently in how bodies encounter the area. Individuals sit on the floor; others stand and sway even when the majority is seated; pews give way to moveable chairs or floor seating; bodies come into contact with each other, moving, touching, and encountering each other during worship. By reconceptualizing the space in this way, worshipers embody a feminist principle of religious agency. Although the group functions as a collective, each individual is able to utilize the space as an individual, moving through the literal space as she feels compelled rather than by following a scripted series of movements which would otherwise keep her in synchronized movement with the rest of the congregation.

This type of tactile synergy is in line with Sklar's (1994) description of embodied interaction during a Purimspiel. She identifies that women in the balcony of an Orthodox synagogue encounter energy through the movement, skin touching, and close proximity, the importance which should not be overlooked because the women are not key players in the "main" event. In the Renewal space, this same type of synergistic group encounter takes place. Although it is not a formalized part of the worship, the proximity of the bodies, how they use the space, and the ways in which bodies physically encounter other bodies is richly important to the overall experience of the religious moment.

Finally, the use of bodies in the Renewal movement is feminist in its acceptance of all bodies. Body acceptance is not to be equated solely with body positivity, although arguably the Renewal movement is also body positive in its goals. Instead, the way in which the body is understood in Renewal spaces celebrates all bodies and demonstrates this through creating accessible experiences. This focus on accessibility includes allowing mothers to breastfeed during worship, creating accessible spaces for differently abled individuals, and celebrating racial and ethnic diversity. It is a body politic that not only celebrates women and their contributions to Jewish life, but works to create environments that allow all women, all men, and all individuals (including those who identify outside of male/female binaries) to worship together. If the worship space is understood to be malleable, it can be changed in ways that are radically hospitable and accepting, allowing everyone a seat in the circle, regardless of her body size, abilities, limitations, or needs. Imagine, for example, the incorporation of an individual who uses a motorized wheelchair into the circle. Rather than marginalizing her by sitting her on the end of a pew or in a specially designated area, the Renewal circle is able to accommodate her without prioritizing her chair over her personhood. In essence, by eliminating the second row, everyone is afforded a first-row seat. At its core, this is a feminist approach to bodies, one that celebrates the individual by including her fully rather than by defining her by terms outside of herself.

In the end, the bodylore of the Jewish Renewal movement is most significant in its potential. That is not to diminish the importance of the work that has already been done, but rather to point to the great potential of the ways in which the body is treated within the movement. The redoing of Judaism in the Renewal movement demonstrates attention to corporality; the body engages spirituality or, at least, engages spiritual performance. In doing so, old meets new and tradition is once again renewed for the next generation. But such a description is too simplistic, as it fails to recognize a fundamental shift in perception: the Renewal movement is more than a neo-Hasidic response, as it works to redo practices in a way that fundamentally shifts the function of folklore and ritual, especially around the body.

A MOVEMENT TO RE-EMBODY JUDAISM

Reb Zalman identifies four axes of the individual: physical, emotional, spiritual, and intellectual (Schachter-Shalomi and Segel 2012, 140). These all come together and coalesce in personhood. This chapter has highlighted the experience of the physical as part of the Renewal experience. In a video where others are learning about ecstatic music at the University of Colorado at Boulder, Reb Zalman entreats the audience, "Will you stand up and stretch so that you are ready to listen to the next section?" (CU Boulder Libraries 2014). For him, these parts of the individual are intrinsically tied together, such that the physical cannot be separated from the spiritual. Unlike other religious teachings that treat the body as a weakness to be overcome, in Reb Zalman's understanding, the physicality of the body is just as important as intellect, emotion, and the spirit. Indeed, it is in our physical bodies that these other aspects of personhood intersect.

By engaging the body in multifaceted ways—from dance and voice to craft and yoga—the Renewal movement opens up space for the body to be centralized in worship in new and exciting ways. Furthermore, it does not place limits on the body, such that all bodies can be present and fully engaged in experiencing Judaism regardless of physical differences. This allows the body to become a feminist text in two ways. First, it is a space for the celebration of identity intersections, uplifting individuals in full personhood. Second, it is not limited by religious conventions. In the redoing of Judaism, the body and the individual are met with options for engaging the whole person. In this holistic approach, Renewal Judaism recognizes not only that bodies are unique but that the spiritual needs of the individual are also different and can be met through different forms of body engagement. Although traditionalists are quick to dismiss the Renewal movement as being "too New Age," and it is true that their approach will not appeal to all Jews, the revolutionary work that they are doing is in re-embodying Judaism. This chapter has engaged Darwin's theory of redoing Judaism and suggested that the Renewal movement is doing just that, but, perhaps even more importantly, what the Renewal movement is doing is re-embodying Jewishness by centering the body again as a space for individuals to encounter and engage Judaism.

The future of the Renewal movement is not clear; but, in an age where Jewish denominations are grappling with how to create inclusive and welcoming environments, there is no need to reinvent the wheel. The Renewal movement has already articulated ways of reimagining Jewish practice. Although their methods may not apply in all congregational contexts, the mainstream Jewish "radical hospitality" movements should look to Renewal for an example. They have demonstrated re-embodiment, showing that the circle of worship, spirituality, and Judaism can expand to include all who wish to join it. As our own ideas of intersectionality expand, so too can the circle expand to include all Jews.

NOTES

1. Tosefta Berachot 3.
2. Zohar to Numbers 218b–219a.
3. Tanya 19.

4. More on Avodah Dance can be found on their website: http://avodahdance.org/. Their work extends beyond interpreting Jewish texts and is a powerful engagement of dance, the body, and social justice work.

5. For more on the Institute of Contemporary Midrash and their community-based trainings and drama residencies, visit: http://www.icmidrash.org/community-based-trainings-residencies/).

6. For more information on Elat Chayyim, visit their website at: https://hazon.org/isabella-freedman/elat-chayyim/.

Chapter Three

Rebellious Hair

Jewish Feminist Reinterpretations of the Orthodox Jewish Ritual of Upsherin

We were sitting at a shared table, chatting over lunch at a professional confer-ence. I had spotted her *yarmulke* and asked her a few questions about it be-cause, as a Jewish bodylorist, I am always curious about how we encode our bodies in non-Jewish spaces. As our conversation progressed, she asked me about my current project and I told her I was investigating feminist *upsherin*. She leaned across the table, placed her hand on my arm, and said, "It was one of the most meaningful things I did for my daughters. They may not remem-ber it but I do, even more than their *bat mitzvahs*." I had struck gold. After months of scrolling through blogs and discussion boards, I had my first "in the flesh" Jewish feminist who had held a feminist *upsherin* for her daughters.

In the following months I would have conversations with several women who hosted feminist *upsherin* rituals for their daughters and as an expression of their own feminist Judaism. In this chapter, I begin by offering a brief overview of the Jewish practice of *upsherin*, followed by a thick description (Geertz 1973) of one feminist *upsherin*. I situate the practice in Jewish ritual studies and Jewish feminism, offer a contextualized analysis of the ritual, and ultimately argue that feminist *upsherin* is a distinct and innovative feminist ritual and not an iteration or adaptation of the Orthodox *upsherin* for boys.

UPSHERIN AS AN ORTHODOX PRACTICE

Upsherin is the Jewish ritual haircutting practice of young boys, generally at the age of three. The practice itself is typically found among the most religiously conservative (sometimes also referred to as "observant") Hasidic, Haredi, and Orthodox communities. The ritual begins with a haircutting cer-emony and is followed by the *alef-bet*, a learning initiation ritual.

Upsherin takes place in either the home or the synagogue. During the ceremony, the young boy enters the ritual space wearing a yarmulke (the traditionally male skullcap worn by Jews, also known as a *kippah* in Hebrew) and *tzitzit* (the knotted ritual fringes traditionally worn by observant Jewish men, typically attached to a four-cornered garment) for the first time. Often holding his son in his lap, the father cuts the first lock of hair on the front of the boy's forehead as a symbolic gesture of where the boy will one day lay *tefillin* (leather boxes holding scripture that are bound to the forehead and left arm). The rest of the hair is cut, many times allowing all in attendance to snip a lock, being careful to retain the hair on the sides of the head, as the ritual creates the boy's *payot* (sidelocks or sidecurls worn by Jewish men, some- times also referred to as *payos* in Yiddish). As is common in American cul- ture, many families preserve the first cut lock of hair, in this case by pressing it between the pages of a prayer book. The rest of the hair is either disposed of or weighed so that a corresponding donation can be made to a charity. Throughout the ritual, there is a theme of *tzedakah* (charitable giving), one of central moral obligations of Jews. In addition to donations being made in correspondence to the weight of the hair or the number of locks snipped, the boy is sometimes given a *tzedakah* box to hold throughout the ritual. Those snipping his hair will place coins or bills into the small box as they cut his hair, and others in attendance may also make contributions which are given, most commonly, to a charity related to Jewish education (Milligan 2017, 12). Other families extend this idea of charitable giving to include donating the hair of the boy to an organization that makes wigs for children with cancer or alopecia (Pinson 2010, 48).

The *upsherin* is commonly paired with the *alef-bet* ritual in the United States. This education initiation marks the beginning of Jewish learning for a young boy. The boy is carried to a male teacher or a rabbi by his father and is wrapped in his father's *tallit* (the prayer shawl traditionally worn by Jewish men, also known as *tallis* in Yiddish). The *alef-bet* can take place in the home, synagogue, *yeshiva* (a Jewish educational institution), or school. Seated on the lap of the male teacher or rabbi, the boy reads the Hebrew alphabet aloud, following the cues given by the teacher. Reading from the beginning to the end and then in reverse, the boy uses his finger on a lami- nated card that is sprinkled with honey. Dipping his finger into the honey on each letter, he is taught that learning is sweet and rewarding (Blau 2003, 185; Milligan 2017, 11–13)

There are many variations of this practice, including taking pilgrimages on Lag B'Omer, how the hair is disposed, the distribution of sweets and candy, the age at which it is performed, and the nuances of performance (from hair bows to body positioning) (Blau 2003, 183–86; Milligan 2017, 13). Regardless of variations in practice, *upsherin* is a significant rite of passage in the lifecycle of Orthodox Jewish boys. It marks the transition from babyhood to childhood, and in doing so establishes a gendered divide between a boy and his mother. A baby enters the ritual and a boy emerges, having now been given a Jewish male identity kit (Goffman 1965) that he may use as a symbolic inventory to encode his body as he learns masculine social performance (see Askew 1998; Bronner 2005; Butler 1990; Kimmel 2009; Miller 2010). In addition, *upsherin* affirms key Jewish values and morals (charitable giving, family, and education), as well as establishes the boy's masculinity and role as a learner and performer of public Jewishness (Goldberg 1987; Milligan 2017, 14–20).

THICK DESCRIPTION: A FEMINIST *UPSHERIN*

Given the patriarchal nature of Orthodox *upsherin*, it is difficult for many non-Orthodox Jews to imagine that the ritual could be anything but male-centered. Still, some liberal Jews have created egalitarian adaptations of the ritual. This chapter, however, considers feminist *upsherin* rituals as distinct from both egalitarian *upsherin* and Orthodox *upsherin*. The feminist *upsherin* is part of a grassroots movement of Jewish women creating a ritual for their daughters in which they use elements of the traditional *upsherin* to challenge patriarchy and to center both the bodies and the voices of their daughters in a community of lovingkindness. The following description is an example of one such practice.

Jill is a thirty-nine-year-old mother of four, three daughters and one son. She identifies as a Reform Jew with a deep interest in the Renewal movement. She has had *upsherin* for all of her children. When asked about her decision to engage with a haircutting ritual, she explained that she learned about the Orthodox practice from reading a Jewish parenting book and discovered feminist *upsherin* in an online message board forum. Jill described how she considered consulting a rabbi but ultimately decided that she had enough Jewish knowledge to create a meaningful ritual on her own.

For the *upsherin* of Olivia, her youngest daughter, Jill invited female friends and family members to participate, fourteen in total. Jill lifted Olivia, dressed in a special party dress, into her booster seat in the kitchen, and the women gathered in a circle around the chair. Maddie and Zoe, Jill's two other daughters, wove between bodies to stand in the front of the circle, facing their sister. Jill instructed the group to hold hands and take a moment to center themselves, focusing on their breathing. She broke the silence to invite each of her daughters to read a short poem that they had written for their sister.

Leaning over to kiss the top of Olivia's head, Jill explained to the group that this ritual was a celebration of the transition to childhood and that Olivia's *upsherin* was an affirmation of Jill's commitment to raising and educating a Jewish daughter; it was also a way to celebrate that, at four years old, Olivia understood the importance of social justice and was developing into her own spirited individuality.

Jill carefully trimmed the first lock of hair from the nape of Olivia's neck, which she preserved by carefully pressing it between the pages of a baby book she kept for each of her children. Following this, she gave instructions that each should snip a small lock of hair, careful not to trim it too short, and place it in the basket her other daughter, Zoe, was holding. As each woman cut Olivia's hair, the guest was instructed to "speak an intention." These intentions included things like "may you grow to be strong and fearless" and "may you seek justice in all of your ways." They also included instructions like "may you not fear those who are different than you" and "may you come to know that you are not defined by beauty." Maddie, Olivia's sister, carefully wrote each of these intentions down in the back of Olivia's baby book, pausing from time to time to ask for spelling clarification.

At the end of the haircutting, Jill gathered the circle together again and spoke a few words read from a notecard; she affirmed her own commitment to ensuring Olivia's access to education and to having nurturing, safe spaces, adding that she loved her daughter fully in all of her "flawed humanity" and would fight for Olivia to always have space for her opinions. Jill then invited those who were familiar with the prayer to chant along with Avot v'Imahot (see table 3.1), the part of the *Amidah* prayer that praises God and the biblical patriarchs and matriarchs.[1]

Maddie and Zoe then proudly helped their youngest sister lead the group in the *Shema* (the centerpiece of Jewish prayer; see table 3.2).

Table 3.1.   Avot v'Imahot

Baruch atah, Adonai Eloheinu v'Elohei avoteinu v'imoteinu, Elohei Avraham, Elohei Yitzchak v'Elohei Yaakov, Elohei Sarah, Elohei Rivkah, Elohei Rachel v'Elohei Leah. Ha-El hagadol hagibor v'hanora, El elyon, gomeil chasadim tovim, v'koneih hakol, v'zocheir chasdei avot v'imahot, umeivi g'ulah liv'nei v'neihem l'maan sh'mo b'ahavah.	Blessed are You, *Adonai* our God, God of our fathers and mothers, God of Abraham, God of Isaac, and God of Jacob, God of Sarah, God of Rebecca, God of Rachel, and God of Leah, the great, mighty and awesome God, transcendent God who bestows lovingkindness, creates everything out of love, remembers the love of our fathers and mothers, and brings redemption to their children's children for the sake of the Divine Name.

Table 3.2. Shema

Sh'ma Yisra'eil Adonai Eloheinu Adonai echad. Barukh scheim k'vod malkhuto l'olam va'ed.	Hear, Israel, the Lord is our God, the Lord is one. Blessed be the name of God's glorious kingdom forever and ever.

The ritual was closed by one final song, a nod to the Hebrew *alef-bet* ritual that typically accompanies Orthodox *upsherin* in American contexts. Olivia sang the English ABCs with a little bit of encouragement and support from her sisters. At the conclusion, Olivia was scooped up and passed between guests, showered with kisses and hugs. The rest of the celebration was akin to a typical American child's birthday party, filled with food, snacks, games, and casual conversation.

Jill admits that she was overly ambitious when she planned her first feminist *upsherin*, including songs like "Free to be You and Me," which guests struggled to sing without musical accompaniment. By the time she had an Olivia's *upsherin*, she had streamlined the ritual and trimmed it to what she identified as the most meaningful elements. When asked if she also had an *upsherin* for her son, Jill said that she had hosted one, but it was different than what she had done for her daughters. It was more in line with an egalitarian *upsherin* than a feminist *upsherin*. Her son's *upsherin* featured male and female guests, as well as more recitation of liturgy and Hebrew. His hair was cut on his third birthday, unlike his sisters who all had their hair cut between the ages of four and five. He also wore a small *yarmulke*, something Jill now regrets because she feels like this action plays into the very religious patriarchy she prides herself on rejecting. The *yarmulke* was a gift from a grandparent, and, at the time, she thought it was cute. Her regret is less about her son wearing the *yarmulke* than it is about the inequality of not offering her daughters the option of religious garb. As she describes it, this difference prompted some family members to comment on how she had a "real" *upsherin* for her son, in contrast to the "made-up" one she had for her daughters.

Jill admits that she doubts that she would have had an *upsherin* for her son if she had not already done so for his older sisters. For her, the feminist *upsherin* is less about the actual haircutting and inherited Jewish symbol set, and more about the centering and empowerment of women's voices. Surrounded by generations of women in the room, regardless of their faith traditions, Jill uses the feminist *upsherin* to create a feminist space for her daughters, an experience that she believes is just as important for her older daughters as it is for the child having her hair cut.

THE CREATION OF JEWISH FEMINIST RITUAL

One of the central questions in feminist ritual discourse has been whether to abandon, dismantle, or reinvent patriarchal structures (Gross 1996). When the lens of religion is placed on this question, feminists grapple with whether or not patriarchy is so entrenched in religions that it cannot be overcome, or if there are ways to work from within religious traditions to subvert authority and redistribute religious power and autonomy in feminist and egalitarian ways (Cooey, Eakin, and McDaniel 1991).

Jewish feminism largely began during the second wave of the American feminist movement (1950–1980). The second wave featured many prominent Jewish women including secular voices like Betty Friedan, Gloria Steinem, Shulamith Firestone, Andrea Dworkin, and Vivian Gornick. As American feminism evolved to take a more intersectional approach, Jewish feminists began to critique the entrenched patriarchy of Judaism (see Cohen 1980; Heschel 1991). Early pivotal works include Trude Weiss-Rosmarin's "The Unfreedom of Jewish Women" (1970) and Rachel Adler's "The Jew Who Wasn't There: Halacha and the Jewish Woman" (1972), which paved the road for Jewish feminist thought. Although, until the early 1970s, much of Jewish feminist discussion focused on the ordination of women, a shift occurred in the dialogue when Jewish women began to further analyze Jewish tradition and practice. As was seen at New York City's 1973 first National Conference on Jewish Women, not only were Jewish feminists interested in the ordination of female clergy, but they also wished to address other inequalities in Jewish tradition, including marriage and divorce laws, counting women toward a *minyan* (the quorum of ten, traditionally men, necessary for Jewish communal prayer), masculine God language, patriarchal liturgy, women's roles in synagogue and public Jewish life, and women's interpretations of Jewish texts (see Fishman 1995; Heschel 1987; Hyman 1995; Levitt 1997; Plaskow 1997; Plaskow 1991; Ruttenberg 2001).

Although the purpose of this chapter is not to trace the development of Jewish feminism, it is important to understand the evolution of Jewish feminist ritual in the context of early Jewish American feminism and its continued impact on how Jewish women understand their role as ritual innovators. As second wave Jewish feminists began to challenge and dismantle the structures of patriarchal Judaism, one of the ways they did this was through engaging ritual. Vanessa Ochs, in *Inventing Jewish Ritual* (2010), identifies two primary forces behind ritual innovation: open access (particularly through catalog Judaism) and Jewish feminism (ibid., 39–52). She explains that as Jewish women became more Jewishly literate and advanced to roles of Jewish leadership, they created a new force for ritual innovation (ibid.,

46). As feminists broached Jewish ritual, Ochs identifies that they have done so using two approaches: either adapting rituals or creating new rituals (ibid., 47). Adaptation, in this case, means that rituals that previously prohibited women's participation (counting toward a *minyan*, wearing ritual garb, performing certain religious tasks) are rendered egalitarian and inclusive of women.

Examples of adaptive rituals include Jewish feminists taking the traditional Passover *Seder* and creating feminist Passover *Seders*. Other examples include parallel rites of passage, including baby name ceremonies for girls (*brit bat* or *simchat bat*, a covenant ceremony for girls, parallel to *brit milah*, the covenantal circumcision ceremony for boys), *pidyon ha-bat* (the redemption of the first born daughter, analogous to *pidyon ha-ben*), and the most familiar example, the evolution of the *bat mitzvah* as a equivalent to the *bar mitzvah* (a Jewish coming of age ritual).

Although, on the surface, adaptive ritual may seem like an adequate egalitarian shift, many Jewish feminists are critical of what Ochs calls an "add women and stir" approach (2010, 47), positing that adaptive rituals still privilege the historical male voice and have not actually been adapted to meet the spiritual or community needs of Jewish women. As a response to this, Jewish feminists have been innovative in their creation of new Jewish rituals. These new rituals center the experiences of women and challenge many traditional Jewish beliefs (e.g., a masculine God, a lack of Jewish spirituality, the sub status of the female body, a heavy focus on Jewish law).

One example of ritual innovation is the celebration of *Rosh Chodesh* (the start of a new Jewish month). Although *Rosh Chodesh* had long been associated with women, both based in Jewish legend as well as in the association of it with the menstrual cycle, it was not until the mid-1980s that it fully entered the Jewish feminist imagination (see Berrin 1998; Novick 2014). Historically women, particularly of Eastern European descent, wrote special *Rosh Chodesh techinos* (personal prayers which were written in Yiddish or the local vernacular) (Baskin 2001, 131; Goldberg 2005); this practice was revitalized in the 1980s when *Rosh Chodesh* groups emerged in the United States as a place for contemplative and creative experiences of Jewish femininity. Penina Adelman describes in *Miriam's Well: Rituals for Jewish Women Around the Year* (1990) how *Rosh Chodesh* groups developed anointing rituals to honor the "messiah in each individual" (ibid., 29) as well as how women are able to use these ritual spaces to address "sexual harassment, low pay, [and] the beauty industry" (ibid., 65). These groups have continued to evolve, including a variety of both religious and secular women, and affording them a space where women can focus on spiritual growth, social activism, discussions of ethics, or textual study.

Other examples of inventive Jewish feminist ritual include the placement of an orange on the *Seder* plate (a somewhat contested symbol, representing LGBTQ Jews as well as women on the *bimah* [Alpert 1998; Milligan 2014]), the *mikveh* ceremony for African American and Jewish women as a cleansing of racism, grief and loss rituals (particularly around the loss of a mother figure), and rituals around breastfeeding, menopause, name changes, divorce, and childbirth (Broner 1999).

At their core, Jewish feminist rituals, whether adaptive or inventive, focus on community transformation. These acts legitimize women's voices and, when done well, also grant space to other marginalized voices, including children, the LGBTQ community, Jews of different abilities, and Jews of Color. By rescripting Jewish ritual to include a variety of Jewish women's voices and experiences, they challenge exclusionary traditions and texts, reinventing ritual in an encompassing and affirming way.

FEMINIST *UPSHERIN* AS INVENTIVE RITUAL

Unlike other rituals and rites of passage that have been adapted by Jewish feminists, *upsherin* has remained largely overlooked. This lack of fully embraced analogous egalitarian ritual highlights the divide between non-Orthodox Jews and Orthodoxy, or at least how non-Orthodox Jews view certain practices as "too" Orthodox. Egalitarian *upsherin*, as practiced by relatively few liberal Jews, often involve a hair stylist, both male and female participants, the honey dipping *alef-bet*, and typically occur at the age of three (see Cooper 2014). In looking for examples of egalitarian *upsherin*, it is more common for liberal Jewish families to have one for their sons than for their daughters. And those that do have an egalitarian *upsherin* often cite higher exposure to or familiarity with Orthodox communities (see Gechter 2015). Why, then, would Jewish feminists take interest in this practice? And is it a practice that can be saved from its patriarchal roots?

First, the initial haircut is an important milestone for parents. Relatively little scholarship has considered the hairlore of infants and very young children, in large part because many of these children do not have stylized hair and, if the child has enough hair to style, decisions about appearance are made by a caregiver. The decisions that adults make about the hair of infants and very small children, though, are significant and largely culturally or religiously based, including the creation of *payot*, rituals around first haircuts, the decision not to cut hair, or choices of the stylization of hair in age or culturally appropriate styles (see Milligan 2017, 8–10).

Hair takes on special significance for small children in how it denotes maturity. The shift from baby to toddler and from toddler to school-aged child is externalized, when hair growth cooperates, by the child's hair. Because of this, a child's first haircut also takes on meaning for caregivers, as it marks the transition from baby to child. In particular, the ritual of the first haircut engages gender in two overt forms. First, the haircut itself marks the shift of the status of the toddler; she is no longer an infant and is now an independent small child. This change in status is congruent with a shift in the mother's role.[2] The baby had been dependent on the mother (breast milk, physical touch, mobility) but now has the independence of a toddler, including learning and being influenced by other adults outside of the immediate family, causing a shift in the primary gendered role of the mother.

Second, the child is gendered externally through the haircut. Although there are a number of ways in which babies are gendered (e.g., clothing, colors, hair bows, toys, names, and the language used to speak to them), one of the first physical manifestations of gender that the child carries on her body is her haircut. Although circumcision marks Jewish boys, it is a private symbol, unlike hair, which is a public symbol that allows others to differentiate children by gender. In fact, Yoram Blau even calls an Orthodox *upsherin* a secondary circumcision, where a boy is once again physically marked and sanctified as a Jew (2003, 187–93).[3] The baby's hair had been allowed to grow freely, without shape or form, and at the first haircut, it is stylized by gendered conventions, usually cut shorter for boys and only trimmed (often only to keep it out of the eyes) for girls. For this reason the first haircut for boys is often earlier than that of girls, or, at minimum, the results of the haircut appear more drastic for boys.

If there is a way to cut the hair of boys Jewishly, is there not also a way to do the same for girls? Why have some women chosen to have a feminist *upsherin* for their daughters and not their sons? More importantly, is feminist *upsherin* actually an adaptation of the Orthodox practice or is it a unique ritual that shares the same name?

In order to assess whether feminist *upsherin* is an adaptive or an inventive ritual, it is helpful to consider the eight characteristics of feminist inventive rituals identified by Ochs: marking the unmarked, fostering community, allowing for improvisation and personalization, privileging the spirituality of the individual over that of the entire Jewish people, taking place in less regulated space, being self-explanatory and easy to use, allowing for spontaneity, and promoting a Jewish women's agenda (Ochs 2010, 48–52). Feminist *upsherin* fits well within this framework:

1. It marks the unmarked in a significant way. Jewish boys are given an externalization of their Jewishness through their circumcision. The adapted parallel ritual of a baby naming ceremony for girls does not have this same

physical change. The feminist *upsherin*, then, is the first time that a Jewish girl is physically marked as Jewish.

2. A feminist *upsherin* fosters community. Like other Jewish feminist rituals, a feminist *upsherin* generally happens with a female audience, bringing together Jews and non-Jews across generations in a moment centered on a female child. This is, quite literally, the village to which feminist circles refer. These are the women who will raise the child.

3. Feminist *upsherin* is not scripted or based on liturgy, allowing for improvisation and personalization. This allows for a range of practices, from songs, poetry, readings, and the use of other liturgical texts. It also creates space for family practices and the incorporation of other traditions (for example, having children involved, using a particular hair comb from a beloved grandmother, or involving favorite secular songs).

4. There is an emphasis on the individual over *klal Yisrael* (all of the Jewish people). In the case of feminist *upsherin*, the focus is on the daughter and of the group of women or the family. One need not have an *upsherin* to partake in any particular aspect of Jewish life. Rather, it is about creating space to focus on the commitment to the spiritual, emotional, physical, and intellectual well-being of the girl.

5. Feminist *upsherin* generally take place in the home and not in regulated spaces. Unlike traditional Orthodox *upsherin*, which often make a move to the synagogue or the *yeshiva*, feminist *upsherin* occur at home and often in the kitchen, as opposed to a formal dining area or living room.

6. The feminist *upsherin* is self-explanatory and accessible to all who are involved. It does not rely heavily on Hebrew (and, if Hebrew is used, it is transliterated and often a familiar prayer or blessing). The event is filled with instruction from the mother, guiding those in attendance through the ritual step-by-step. The space is that of familiarity: the language used, the physical location, the casual dress. All who are in attendance are equally able to take part in the ritual, regardless of their own religious beliefs or education.

7. The timing of the feminist *upsherin* allows for spontaneity. The first haircut does not have to take place on the girl's third birthday, but rather whenever her hair is ready to be cut. Because it is tied to another rite of passage or calendar date, the feminist *upsherin* occurs when the caregivers deem it appropriate or when the hair is long enough. Furthermore, the ritual itself also allows for another form of spontaneity with the inclusion of children. Young children are unpredictable. Sometimes the party has to happen before the haircutting because the girl is still napping. Other times desperate siblings beg to have their hair cut, too. Feminist *upsherin*

embraces these as aspects of family life, allowing the unexpected to seamlessly weave into the larger ritual scene.

8. Finally, feminist *upsherin* promotes a Jewish women's agenda. The heart of the ritual rests in the commitment to creating space for the Jewish female voice. The ritual is just as much for the mother, acknowledging her shifting role in the life of the baby, as it is for the daughter, indicating that she will be afforded space to cultivate her own experience of Judaism and supported by a community of women.

Although feminist *upsherin* meets all of the criteria identified by Ochs as indicators of inventive ritual, by virtue of its name, some might still consider it an adaptation of the Orthodox male ritual. Both commemorate the first haircut and are a public affirmation of the commitment to raising a child Jewishly. However, the two are fundamentally different. Feminist *upsherin* does not create an analogous ritual in the same way that a bar and *bat mitzvah* are parallel. Rather, it is its own inventive and unique Jewish ritual. This can be seen through consideration of the symbol set utilized and of the ritual's intentions.

First, an Orthodox *upsherin* encompasses three central themes: the boy taking on a Jewish identity kit (*yarmulke*, *tzitzit*, *payot*, and eventually, as symbolized by his father's actions, *tefillin* and a *tallis*), the separation of the boy from his mother, and the commitment to the boy's Jewish learning. A feminist *upsherin* does not engage this same symbolic inventory. The girl is not wrapped in a prayer shawl, nor does she wear *tzitzit* or a *yarmulke*. Some women in attendance might choose to wear these items, but the emphasis is not on the creation of an external Jewishness for the child but rather on cultivating her inward spiritual Jewishness. The focus is also not on the transition of baby from maternal care, but rather on the transition from baby to child, with the mother retaining the central role in the child's life. And, finally, there is less of an emphasis on Jewish learning, which is replaced with a commitment to nurturing a spiritual individual. The focus is not on the literal "letter of the law" and instead on the holistic idea of committing to raise a child as part of a supportive network of caregivers. In the Orthodox *upsherin* the individuals responsible for education are all male and designated as official educators, including teachers and the *Rebbe* (a rabbi or teacher or mentor who is ordained; within Hasidism, refers to the leader of the movement). In the feminist *upsherin*, there is an affirmation of the potential for learning from all of the women surrounding the child. These uncredentialed educators will teach the girl in informal ways, as role models, caregivers, nurturers, and cheerleaders.

Second, the intention of the ritual is fundamentally different. At the Orthodox *upsherin*, the boy inherits Jewish male symbols that were never contested, as they were always symbols for his use. The entire ritual undergirds the inherited power of religious patriarchy, in which the boy's experiences of the community predicate his maleness. The community-based ritual affirms gender roles: the Rebbe at the center, flanked by the male teacher, the father and son, and male guests. On the sidelines, largely uninvolved in the ritual scene, are the mother, the daughters, and other female guests. The entire ritual reaffirms the patriarchal hierarchy of the community, with each guest playing his or her gendered role.

In contrast, the feminist *upsherin* subverts the hierarchy. The central figure controlling the ritual is the mother. But the mother's role is to lead the group through the ritual, not to dictate the ritual performance, which allows for the voices of participants to carry equal weight (for example in the readings offered by siblings or in the intentions spoken by guests). Rather than inheriting a symbolic inventory, the daughter inherits a community of women to nurture her. The intention is not to replicate the authority of the synagogue in the ritual space, but rather to demonstrate an intensely spiritual and interconnected experience of Judaism, one that exists separate from formal religious spaces and structures.

Ultimately, the Orthodox *upsherin* and the feminist *upsherin* are two distinct rituals. Although they share certain elements (haircutting and, in some cases, the recitation of the alphabet), feminist *upsherin* is not an adaptation of Orthodox *upsherin*. As it is currently performed, the feminist *upsherin* utilizes the familiar action of haircutting and the ABCs as a way of legitimizing a female-centered ritual for young girls. Ochs describes a "Jewish ritual toolbox" in her explorations of inventing new Jewish rituals. This toolbox includes texts, familiar Jewish ritual actions and objects, and Jewish core values. When inventing new rituals, the toolbox can be used for inspiration and guidance (Ochs 2010, 5–7). In the case of feminist *upsherin*, the ritual innovators use the tools of the actions and objects to make the ritual feel both Jewish and sacred. Ochs notes that "borrowing from within Jewish culture [makes] the ritual feel as if it is already 'ours,' and genuinely Jewish, even if we have never heard of it before," which in turn "evokes certainty, security, and imagined community" (ibid., 6).

The borrowed elements, including even the word *upsherin*, should not detract from the inventiveness of the feminist *upsherin*. The same way that other elements are shared between rituals (prayers, texts, body positioning, candle lighting, and objects like the *shofar* [a ram's horn]), feminist *upsherin* utilizes the element of haircutting to substantiate the Jewishness of the ritual for young girls. In using familiar words (*upsherin*) and actions (haircutting, singing the Shema), the feminist ritual feels Jewish but unlike Orthodox *upsherin*, the ritual is about female spirituality and communities of women raising girls.

THE FUTURE OF FEMINIST *UPSHERIN*

A test of whether feminist *upsherin* is an invention or an adaptation of the Orthodox *upsherin* is the potential for analogous rituals for boys. Orthodox rabbis are clear, their perceived female parallel to *upsherin* is Sabbath candle lighting instruction. But if feminist *upsherin* is its own distinct ritual, what is the analogous potential ritual for boys?

An easy answer to this question would be to look to Orthodox *upsherin*. This provides a framework for male *upsherin*, one steeped in tradition and, of course, patriarchy. A liberal egalitarian adaption of Orthodox *upsherin* for boys, as has been practiced by a growing number of non-Orthodox Jews, includes boys having their hair cut, wearing a *yarmulke* for the first time, and reciting the Hebrew alphabet with an adult. On the surface, it seems innocuous, but it highlights the fundamental differentiation of Orthodox *upsherin* and feminist *upsherin* as distinct rituals.

If this liberal adaptation of Orthodox *upsherin* were the analogous parallel, the ritual falls into the same trap as other adapted rituals. It creates the "real" *upsherin* for boys and the "modified" version for girls. The other issue for liberal Jews is, of course, that most do not wear *payot*, nor do they engage regularly with the other identity kit symbols (*yarmulke, tzitzit, tallis, tefillin*). Still, these symbols retain their maleness even when used in the liberal egalitarian *upsherin*, like they do during other life cycle events (for example when a groom wears a *yarmulke, kittel,* or *tallis* but the bride does not), further undergirding the male-centered public performance of Judaism.

If the feminist *upsherin* is to be adapted for a son, how would it differ? First, the mother or primary caregiver would remain at the center of the ritual. Second, the emphasis would remain on the change in the status from baby to child, highlighting the new agency of the child as a thinker, learner, and spiritual being. And finally, and perhaps most importantly, the core of community caregiving would remain central to the ritual. The focus would not be on Jewish learning but rather on embodying a personal Jewish spirituality; the emphasis would not be on public performance of Jewishness but rather on living out the social justice values of Judaism; the role of central authoritative figure is eclipsed by the importance of a community of care.

Throughout many conversations and extensive social media and web searching, I have not yet encountered women who feel strongly about having a feminist *upsherin* for their sons. I have found women who have had liberal egalitarian adaptations of the Orthodox *upsherin* ritual for their sons, although most have not had analogous rituals for their daughters. For the mothers with whom I spoke, their choice to have a feminist *upsherin* for their daughters is a way of creating space and agency for young female bodies. In a religious tradition that still feels patriarchal, and one in which they feel their sons' bodies remain centralized, this is a tangible way of committing to both the bodies and the spirits of their daughters.

The feminist *upsherin* is a tender moment between mother and daughter, one witnessed and enhanced by a community of women. The young girl, seated in the center of a circle of women, is a vessel of promise. She is the next generation of Jewish women and she will be the future voice and body of Jewish feminism. And in this moment, surrounded by generations of other women, they affirm their commitment to raising her, creating space for her, and listening to her voice.

NOTES

1. In non-egalitarian liturgy the matriarchs are omitted, but Jill references the Reform *Siddur*. It is interesting that Jill truncates the *Amidah* (a central Jewish prayer) in this way, but she clarified that it was in an effort to ensure that her guests not feel like they were in a synagogue service. She also noted that saying the names of the matriarchs is meaningful to her, so she selected this portion of the prayer because it resonates with her as a mother.

2. I recognize that the dichotomy of mother/father is problematic and heteronormative and that families do not necessitate two parents. Many loving, healthy, and supportive families do not fit into this traditional framework. I use the mother/father coupling as a means of exploring traditional gendered division, not as a means of being exclusionary. I have attempted to negotiate this by using words like parent and caregiver when appropriate, unless explicitly trying to probe traditional gendered parenting roles.

3. Blau identifies a parallel between *milah* (circumcision) and *milah* (the word), offering a rhetorical argument that *upsherin* is about a secondary circumcision and repurification of the boy's body as he moves away from his mother's breast.

Chapter Four

The *Rosa Winkel*

Jewish Navigation of the Reappropriation of a Nazi Symbol by LGBTQ Young Adults

I remember the moment vividly: among the picked over items for sale at a local Pride festival were several religious items. The rainbow Star of David stickers were sold out, and all of the pride *yarmulkes* were gone. However, a full stack of stickers remained, each emblazoned with a Star of David created by transposing a rainbow and a pink triangle. I stood there and contemplated the sticker. Why hadn't it sold? Was it a case of being misunderstood or was the introduction of the pink triangle on a religious item offensive, especially on Jewish ephemera? The well-meaning teenager manning the table attempted to close the sale, even going so far as to show me his pink triangle tattoo. Later, while reflecting on this moment, I was struck by the strong gut reaction that I had to seeing the pink triangle on a religious item, a much different reaction than I had toward rainbow-colored items in the same context. Familiar with their early use in the gay rights movement, I began to look with renewed interest for pink triangles and observed their increasing popularity, especially among the younger LGBTQ community, begging the question, why has the pink triangle gained recent importance and how has it been reframed by a new generation? In this chapter I offer a brief overview of the history of the *Rosa Winkel*, the pink triangle, tracing its usage from Hitler's Europe to the formation of the American gay rights movement. I analyze contemporary use of the symbol, with particular attention to the tension that exists between perceptions of empowerment versus victimization. I conclude that the pink triangle is a natural folkloric response by young LGBTQ adults who find voice through the symbol by subversively using it to construct a sense of shared community history and mission.

THE ROSA WINKEL:
THE LEGACY OF A HOLOCAUST SYMBOL

Often overlooked when discussing the Holocaust is the persecution and genocide of non-Jewish populations, including the intellectually and physically
disabled, the Roma, Jehovah's Witnesses, criminals, Communists, and others
labeled "asocials" (Berenbaum 1990). Included in this systematic persecution
was also anyone perceived as gay. Less familiar than the iconic yellow Star
of David, the Rosa Winkel, a pink triangle, was used in concentration camps
to identify gay male prisoners. With a flat top and the point straight down, it
was affixed most commonly to the breast of the man's forced uniform, often
on the same badge that identified the individual's assigned concentration
camp number (Grau and Shoppmann 2013). In some cases, a pink and a yellow triangle were arranged together to create a Star of David, thus identifying
a prisoner as both gay and Jewish, someone who was twice marginalized, a
practice that would also be done with other dual identities (e.g., an overlapping yellow and black star for Jewish "asocials" or green and yellow for Jewish criminals) (see Plant 2011).

Early Nazi classification marking systems marked gay prisoners with a
yellow stripe emblazoned with "A," an abbreviation of "Arschficker" (lit.
Assfucker), a black dot, or 175 (a reference to Paragraph 175 of the German
criminal code) (Haeberle 1981, 280–82). This would later evolve into the
pink triangle, the shape of which mirrored other Nazi classification symbols
and the color which was to signal the perceived effeminacy of the gay man
(Haeberle 1981, 284).

Male homosexuality was made explicitly illegal in Paragraph 175 of the
German criminal code, although it was not strictly enforced prior to the Third
Reich, as can be seen by the flourishing gay cultural scenes in cities like Berlin (Whisnant 2016). As part of the "moral crusade" to purify Germany, gay
men were targeted as inherently weak or unfit for the Aryan population (Haeberle 1981, 280; Lautmann 1981). It is estimated that at least 100,000 men
were arrested because of their sexuality, and half were sentenced to prison.
Additionally, between 5,000–15,000 gay men were sent to concentration
camps; it remains unknown how many survived (Jensen 2002; Plant 2011).

The Third Reich was less interested with lesbians, who were not regarded
as a direct threat. However, some women were arrested and sent to concentration camps where they were forced to wear the black triangle, that was used to
mark "asocials," as the pink triangle was used exclusively to mark their gay
male counterparts (Elman 1996; Schoppmann 1996).[1]

In addition to targeting individuals, gay persecution in Nazi Germany also
targeted organizations or places known for their acceptance of gay men. For

example, on May 6, 1933, the Institute for Sexual Science in Berlin was de-
stroyed, including its library (Haeberle 1981, 273). This early incident sent
a strong message of the impending destruction, including the closing of bars
and clubs, the banning of publications (including the popular *Die Freund-
schaft*), and the creation of terror for the gay community (Whisnant 2016).
Through these actions, gay culture was driven underground, causing the Ge-
stapo to encourage local police forces to develop "pink lists" of gay men who
could be investigated and arrested. Reinforced by a 1935 revision of Paragraph 175, which expanded sexual deviance to include any act that could be
considered homosexual including thought or intent even if not enacted, police
continued raiding gay meeting places, began seizing address books (both as
incriminating evidence and to expand their pink lists), and went undercover
to arrest suspected gay men (Haeberle 1981, 275; Kaczorowski 2013).

Once at concentration camps, gay men remained targets. Marked by their
pink triangles, they often were beaten and subject to constant ridicule. Unlike
Jews, who were considered genetically inferior, it was believed that homosexuality was a disease or sickness that was chosen or could be cured. Gay
concentration camp victims were separated and segregated to keep their "disease" from spreading to other inmates and guards. Because of this, they were
given the deadliest of tasks to complete, had experiments performed on their
bodies, and typically existed in isolation from other gay prisoners. Unlike
other targeted groups, who could rely on each other for support, gay prisoners
often found themselves alone and trying to mitigate brutality by befriending
their abusers. As such, some negotiated castration deals, in which they agreed
to castration to "cure" their "sexual deviance" in return for a lesser sentence.
Other prisoners did not choose castration, but were forced to be castrated or to
endure other (usually deadly) medical experimentation on their bodies (Grau
and Shoppman 2013; Haeberle 1981, 282; Lautmann 1981; Plant 2011).

THE PINK TRIANGLE:
REIMAGINING A HOLOCAUST SYMBOL

Although the Rosa Winkel was a stigmatizing and oppressive symbol, less
than thirty years after the Holocaust, the 1970s American gay rights movement readapted and reclaimed the pink triangle. The interest and awareness
of the symbol is likely in part due to the popularity of Heinz Heger's 1970
novel, *Die Männer mit dem Rosa Winkel* (The Men with the Pink Triangle).
In this poignant memoir, the experiences of the gay men during the Holocaust
are detailed—voices which has previously been largely ignored. Three years
after Heger's publication, San Francisco's *Gay Journal* utilized the pink

triangle as a symbol commemorating a legacy of queer persecution (Jensen 2002, 328), which helped the symbol to gain a foothold with other journals and organizations. In 1975, Ira Glasser wrote in the *New York Times* that the Rosa Winkel should be worn to raise awareness and ensure that the gay community not live through another Holocaust. The same imagery would later be evoked by Harvey Milk in a 1978 campaign speech, when he said, "We are not going to sit back in silence as 300,000 of our gay brothers and sisters did in Nazi Germany. We are not going to allow our rights to be taken away and then march with bowed heads into the gas chambers" (Jensen 2002, 329–30; Milligan 2013, 81). Although Milk references both men and women in his speech, early US LGBTQ rights movements are undergirded by a narrative that is gay-normative and steeped in other forms of privilege like race, class, ableism, and cisnormativity. Although problematic in its narrowness, it speaks to the cultural and generational context and is a legacy that contemporary queer movements are both indebted to while simultaneously obligated to dismantle and reimagine.

The early LGBTQ rights movement was profoundly affected by the AIDS epidemic, both in the direct impact of the devastating death toll as well as in the mobilization of a movement around a shared cause (France 2017; Schilts 2007). Because of this, the gay rights movement, the AIDS crisis, and rise in use of the Rosa Winkel are intrinsically linked together. With the crushing mortality caused by AIDS, the 1980s were a time of gay mobilization. Looking directly at death, it is no surprise that the queer community sensed kinship with victims of genocide. As Stuart Marshall describes, ". . . [the] genocide of homosexuals provided us with a group identity similar to that of the Jews. The pink triangle expressed our commonality as victims. . . . Hasn't history repeated itself? Have we not found ourselves again faced by the genocidal actions of a fascist state?" (1991, 85–86).

This Holocaust imagery functioned on three levels. First, the gay community was held culpable for AIDS, as can be seen through the original name of the disease GRID (Gay-Related Immune Deficiency) (Hunter 2006). Much as the Jews and other groups were blamed and targeted in Nazi Germany, the gay community was further stigmatized through this blame. At a time when the community was ravaged by death, they were simultaneously held responsible for their own struggle.

Second, the persecution enforced by the Nazi state paralleled the lack of government support for AIDS research and medical support. The gay rights movement during the AIDS epidemic is a modern civil rights movement, one that is often overlooked as such. The Reagan Administration, in holding to its federal budget cuts, was slow to recognize the epidemic or to fund crucial research or medical intervention. Furthermore, the National Institutes of Health was slow and generally unresponsive to pleas for support from the Centers for Disease Control. Groups like ACT UP (AIDS Coalition to Unleash Power) mobilized to protest the inaccessibility and excessively high costs of AIDS and HIV treatments. As a social justice movement, gay rights focused on addressing pharmaceutical profiteering, the FDA's enactment of long drug approval timelines, the Center for Disease Control's exclusion of women or drug users from AIDS classification, the National Institutes of Health slow reaction to the AIDS epidemic, the underrepresentation of women and people of color in clinical trials, and governmental funding of war and other initiatives while simultaneously claiming a lack of funding for AIDS research (Batza 2018; France 2017; Gould 2009; Jones 2017). The parallel to the Nazi State's oppressive and exclusionary policies resonated deeply with gay activists.

Third, those with AIDS found themselves stigmatized, feared, and quarantined while they faced a terrifying fate. This created parallels to the images and stories of those persecuted during the Holocaust, who also were forced to suffer, were separated from their previous lives, and were aware each day of the fragility of their existence. In the face of certain death, the shared feelings of marginalization and stigmatization created easy parallels to the images of concentration camp victims. Even the literal wasting away of the body mirrored a shared physical plight (see De Lange et al. 2006; Yingling 1997).

THE EVOLUTION OF A QUEER SYMBOLIC INVENTORY

As the gay rights movement formed (and at this time the focus was still very much on cisgender gay men at the exclusion of other identities), the community was faced with a very real problem—how could a community define itself without shared roots? Unlike other groups, where ethnic background, religion, common ideologies, or social class are identifiers that enable group cohesion, the LGB communities share only the experience and subsequent stigma of same-gender attraction, which does not account for asexuality, gender identity, gender expression, or other queer identities. That is to say, the idea of a shared queerness is complicated by the struggle to incorporate a full spectrum of experiences of attraction, identity, gender, sex, and sexuality. In this way, the queer community has struggled with the same issues of the feminist movement. Both movements grew out of the pursuit of social justice, but their initial driving forces were steeped in privilege (Hurtado 1996). Much as third wave feminism has pushed back against its white, heteronormative, cisnormative, socioeconomic, and cultural privileged roots by working to center the voices of *all* women, queer activists continue to work toward evolving a more encompassing understanding of LGBTQ+ identities, issues, and needs (Davis 2008; Mohanty 2003; Narayan 2000). In doing so, they recognize that the movements of the 1980s and their continued narrative prioritize the voices of gay white men at the expense of those fighting alongside them (see Marcus 1992). Still, even with the privileged face of the 1980s queer community, how could the community form under one shared symbol that would be inclusive of all members and their identities?

Initially a variety of symbols were considered. Jim Owls, who was at the time the president of New York's Gay Activist Alliance (GAA), describes that in January 1970 the organization considered several different symbols, including a fighting cock (deemed offensive for lesbians) and the lambda. The lambda, representing "total energy—activism without waste," was chosen as the official GAA logo (Katz 1989, 29), and would go on to be declared the international symbol for LGBTQ rights by the International Gay Rights Congress in 1974 (Zimmerman 1999, 747). Although still used within the queer community, the lambda has been eclipsed by other more commonly used symbols. Even more than a symbol, its name holds rhetorical queer recognition, for example with groups like Lambda Legal or the American Lambda Literary Foundation.

Similar to the lambda, several other symbols were used in the early queer rights movement. Because of its association with matriarchal warriors, the *labrys* (a double-bladed axe) has been symbolically used to represent both the lesbian and the feminist communities since the 1970s. The purple hand was also briefly popular as a unifying symbol. After the Bloody Friday of the Purple Hand on October 31, 1969, when sixty members of the Gay Liberation Front and the Society for Individual Rights gathered outside of the *San Francisco Examiner*'s office to protest a series of homophobic articles, they were assaulted. Their peaceful protest quickly escalated after printers' ink was dumped onto the crowd, which they subsequently used to stamp purple handprints on the walls of the building and surrounding structures (Stryker and Van Buskirk 1996). Although the symbol resonated with community members, its association with violence and "The Black Hand" methods used by the mafia as a scare tactic thwarted its popularity (Sifakis 2005, 43).

In addition to the purple hand, there are numerous other symbols tested, embraced, and used by various LGBTQ groups. They include the black triangle, various interlocking gender symbols, the butterfly, the purple rhinoceros, Sappho, the nautical star, the rooster, the red AIDS ribbon, and the dolphin. Likewise, lavender continues to be associated with the LGBTQ community, having replaced mauve as the symbolic color used in the 1950s–1960s (Jay and Young 1978). Much like the lambda, the word lavender has become perhaps even more important than the literal color, appearing in phrases and names like the Lavender Scare, lavender graduation ceremonies, lavender proms, a lavender marriage, the Lavender Dragon Society, *Lavender* magazine, lavender linguistics, and the Lavender Family Resource Network.

Insider symbols, including the tattooing of things like the blue nautical star on the wrist, the wearing of lambda necklaces, and the utilization of handkerchief code to signal sexual preferences (ranging from partners to roles) (Reilly and Saethre 2013), remain important within the queer community. The most prominent symbol utilized as both an insider and outsider symbol is the rainbow, which evolved later than the aforementioned symbols. On June 25, 1978, Gilbert Baker designed a pride flag for the San Francisco Gay Freedom Day Parade. Initially made with eight stripes (pink for sexuality, red for life, orange for healing, yellow for the sun, green for nature, blue for art, indigo for harmony, and violet for spirit), the flag engaged many of the colors previously used to define the queer community, including the pink of the Rosa Winkel, the green used during Victorian England to symbolize homosexuality, and lavender. The first rainbow flag was handmade by Baker and thirty volunteers, who hand-stitched and hand-dyed the fabric. When Baker subsequently took the flag to have it mass-produced for the 1979 Gay Freedom Day Parade, the pink stripe was removed because it was not a commercially available color (Heinz 2002).

The flag's popularity quickly spread nationwide, especially after the assassination of Harvey Milk on November 27, 1978. The rainbow design of the flag has been utilized and replicated in countless ways, making it the most overtly identifiable contemporary symbol of the LGBTQ community. Similarly, other striped flags have evolved to represent various identity groups within the queer community, including the Bear Pride flag (with a bear print and brown/black colors), and color specific flags for the trans (blue, pink, white), gender queer (lavender, white, green), pansexual (magenta, yellow, blue), bisexual (magenta, lavender, blue), asexual (black, gray, white, purple), and BDSM (black and blue, often with a heart) communities.

During this same time period of the late 1970s through the early1980s, the pink triangle emerged as an alternate symbol to the pride rainbow. In contrast to the unifying pride exemplified by the rainbow, the pink triangle symbolically represented a common historical narrative of queerness and the resulting social injustice, linking the persecution of gay prisoners during the Holocaust to the devastation of the AIDS epidemic. This type of identification is familiar to how social psychologists identify ways in which oppressed groups construct commonality by taking the tools of the oppressor, for example, pejorative language, and reinventing it to reclaim power (Marshall 1991, 91–93; McLeer 1998). By embodying an oppressed status and empowering the identities that are being oppressed, individuals subvert systems of power.

More familiar examples of this include the reclamation by some communities of words like "black," "nigga," "queer," "butch," "dyke," "bitch," and "Chicana," which also create insider-outsider language of who can use the words and in which context, as the words, depending on their usage and speaker, can be empowering or can be a source of violence (Beaton and Washington 2015; Bianchi 2014; Croom 2014). In line with the reclamation of stigmatizing words, the pink triangle has been reclaimed by the LGBTQ community in ways that have enabled the symbol to take on a significant role in which it functions as the keystone to center a community on a shared ideological history. That is to say, the symbol itself is significant, but perhaps even more important is the ideological history that it establishes for a community comprising so many unique identities.

The pink triangle is used both on its own as incorporated into other symbols. For example, it often is used as part of stylized logos; it is sometimes surrounded by a green circle to indicate LGBTQ safe zones, and it is also used in the branding of national LGBTQ organizations like the Brethren Mennonite Council for LGBT Interests, ACT UP (Aids Coalition to Unleash Power), and the Pink Pistols (a queer gun rights organization). The pink triangle also features in art, including Keith Haring's iconic images, designer Orlando Soria's *Hommemaker* fireplace design, and the stained glass of St. Virgil Church in Morris Plains, New Jersey (where God is depicted with a pink triangle halo and outstretched arms).

The pink triangle is also used as a rhetorical phrase. Examples of this include San Francisco's Pink Triangle Park, the Twin Peaks Pink Triangle Ceremony, the Pink Triangle Press, the PT Foundation for HIV/AIDS, and the Pink Triangle Services Centre for the Celebration of Sexual and Gender Diversity. Likewise, the pink triangle has taken on meaning as urban slang and is used as verb, "to be pink triangle," to describe the experience of a man being rejected by a woman whom he did not realize was a lesbian. The phrase strengthened its cultural foothold when it appeared in the band Weezer's song, "The Pink Triangle," which tells listeners "I'm dumb, she's a lesbian. . . . a pink triangle on her sleeve let me know the truth" (Milligan 2013, 79–80).

This reinterpretation of a Holocaust symbol has received mixed responses. Erik Jensen, in his study of the pink triangle, collected responses where critics wrote that using the pink triangle "is indefensible" (Jensen 2002, 319). Members of the Facebook group "LGBTs & FRIENDS Against the Misuse of the Pink Triangle" identify one of their primary goals as getting the LGBTQ community "to stop using the Pink Triangle as a sign of pride, instead of what it is, a sign of persecution, and as such it should be respected to the fullest." The site goes on to write that using the pink triangle is like "a Jewish person putting there [*sic*] relatives [*sic*] Holocaust numbers that were inscribed on

there [*sic*] bodies by Hitler on there [*sic*] business cards to tell possible mer-
chants there [*sic*] Jewish." They conclude by expressing the desire for "young
LGBTs to know where "OUR" people have been (LGBTs n.d.)."[2]

Still, others feel strongly that reimagining the pink triangle "compels us
to take action against homophobic trends, such as the current attempts to
pass antigay initiatives throughout the country" (LGBTs n.d.; Milligan 2013,
80). The contemporary use of the pink triangle, or any Holocaust symbol, is
particularly troubling for many Jews. The Holocaust, at large, has taken on
significant symbolism beyond its history (Poole 2010), and its legacy is used
to create many contemporary narratives, including the parallel of the experiences of Jews and the LGBTQ community (see Novick 2000).

As a community forced to define its shared history around collective
queerness, the LGBTQ historic narrative, unsurprisingly, finds voice through
Holocaust symbolism. Furthermore, as troubling as it is for older LGBTQ
generations, for many contemporary queer youth the AIDS epidemic is not
a formative part of their concept of queer identity and culture. Interestingly,
many seem more familiar with the persecution of gay prisoners during the
Holocaust, suggesting that their Holocaust awareness is heightened due to
exposure in school, whereas LGBTQ history is absent from most curriculums.
In these cases, as was found in Jensen's study, non-Jewish LGBTQ adults
identify the Rosa Winkel as "the proudest symbol that homosexuals can put
forward" (Jensen 2002, 346), articulating a sense of pride in the bravery of
the gay prisoners of the Holocaust which seems in line with other American
romantic notions of the Holocaust. In contrast, the Jews interviewed by Jensen
generally articulated that the pink triangle has "a negative effect of burden-
ing its wearer with a sense of perpetual victimhood" (Ibid., 347). Gay Jews,
especially, seem sensitive to this dual victim identity, both in identifying as
queer and as Jewish, and struggle with utilizing the pink triangle as a positive
symbol or as one emblematic of pride and not victimhood (see Milligan 2013).

In response to these critiques, Jonathan Ned Katz explains that "by dis-
playing a pink triangle as an act of resistance, we transform a Nazi badge
of shame into its opposite: a memorial to the anonymous homosexuals slain
in hate. It is our symbolic marker of our solidarity with all those who fight
injustice" (Katz 1989, 29). Furthermore, for queer teens and young adults,
the Holocaust and even the AIDS epidemic are only pages in a history book.
They are distanced not only by time but also by the lack of survivor's tes-
timony. Further compounding the generational distance, unlike Holocaust
survivors, many of whose oral histories are preserved and taught as part of
high school and college curriculum, the voices of the AIDS epidemic remain
largely silenced. Although some recent work has made progress in capturing
their experiences, the transmission of their legacy is tragically minimal.

In 2015 the popular retail chain Urban Outfitters received criticism for marketing a blue and white stripped tapestry emblazoned with a pink triangle (Anti Defamation League 2017; Sieczkowski 2017), which was on the heels of a 2012 scandal where they sold a yellow shirt with a blue six-pointed star on the breast pocket. Whether these images were used deliberately or not, it is clear that consumers have a sense of "where the line is" in the replication of the symbols. And while young adults, the target consumer of Urban Outfitters, boycotted these items, other uses of the symbol, especially tattoos, have interestingly increased in popularity. Despite the potential ethical conflict of tattooing a Holocaust symbol on the body, these pink triangle tattoos are placed in a variety of areas. It seems especially popular to tattoo the symbol on the wrist, hearkening back perhaps to the use of the blue nautical star wrist-tattoo by the American lesbian community between 1920–1940. The combination of tattooing and a Holocaust symbol is problematic for older Jewish generations but does not appear to create the same dissonance for young adults.

THE PINK TRIANGLE AS
A CONTEMPORARY FOLKLORIC RESPONSE

This reinvigoration of this symbol begs the question, why has the pink triangle gained prominence for queer youth, especially given its generational and cultural distance from the Holocaust and the AIDS epidemic? In order to address this question, it is helpful to consider the pink triangle folklorically. In line with William Bascom's four primary functions of folklore (1954), the contemporary reclamation of the pink triangle will be assessed in terms of its ability to validate culture, its ability to engage narratives of societal repression, as a means of reinforcing cultural values through teaching others, and as a form of social control.

First, the pink triangle legitimizes the queer community's cultural and social experiences. Throughout this text, I have made reference to the LGBTQ community and have hinted at the vast array of personal histories and identities included within the acronym: sex, gender, sexuality, race, education, socioeconomics, ability, religion, and limitless other overlapping identities. In the end, the only thing that the LGBTQ community truly shares is a common queerness. Simply put, the LGBTQ community has as much in common as the heterosexual community.

Much like the pride rainbow symbolizes the spectrum of the LGBTQ community, the pink triangle is malleable enough that it can expand to incorporate the entire spectrum of queerness, although both symbols have roots in the cisgender gay male experience. For young Americans, the rainbow carries a strong association with public personal identity. In contrast, the pink triangle functions as a less overt symbol. It is not as familiar as the rainbow, especially outside of the queer (and arguably the Jewish) community, thereby allowing it to function as insider-language. Similarly, the symbology of the rainbow has been utilized both as a symbol of pride as well as an indicator of support for the LGBTQ community. The commodification of the rainbow has led to it being utilized by allies of the LGBTQ community, who do not identify as queer themselves. While this utilization is not necessarily wrong, it has caused symbolic dilution in its widespread and non-queer-identified usages. The pink triangle, in contrast, is more explicitly used by members of the LGBTQ community, creating a legitimization of a specifically queer identified social and cultural narrative.

In contrast to the easily recognizable pride rainbow, the pink triangle acknowledges the existence of LGBTQ culture through a queer lens. That is to say, early LGBTQ activism and culture felt underground and countercultural. The commodification of queerness, especially through pride or rainbow items, largely overlooks the painful and revolutionary past of the queer community. The pink triangle, at least for those who are fluent in queer culture, gives voice to a shared legacy of existing on the margins, of overcoming violence, and of creating chosen family and queer culture in infertile soil. For LGBTQ youth, it is a "throwback" to the queer activism of the 1980s and a tangible connection to the historic persecution of the LGBTQ community.

Second, this perception of a connection to societal repression through a symbol is key to the rise of the popularity of the pink triangle. Its initial reappropriation after the Holocaust coincided with the rise of the American gay rights movement, largely stemming from a reaction to the onset of the AIDS epidemic. Falling in popularity during the 1990s and early 2000s, the pink triangle has recently made a resurgence in the United States. It seems hardly a coincidence that its resurrection came at a time when the LGBTQ community remobilized in pursuit of marriage equality. Folk symbols, in this case, help mitigate feelings of societal or cultural repression, and the pink triangle functions as an interesting counterbalance to the pride rainbow.

In 2000 Vermont became the first state to recognize civil unions between gay or lesbian couples, paving the way for marriage equality in the United States and the legalization of same-sex marriage in Massachusetts in 2004 and the 2015 United States Supreme Court ruling in *Obergefell v. Hodges*, which ruled that state-level bans on same-sex marriage are unconstitutional. That is not to say that in the years since the AIDS epidemic that the LGBTQ rights movement was inactive. Although same-sex marriage has been an issue for activists since the 1970s, it has been largely since the 1996 passage of the Defense of Marriage Act and subsequent state actions that activists took a more public and vocal role. Although there are certainly a great number of social justice issues that need attention, the right to marry emerged as the most widely discussed and addressed millennial LGBTQ cause.

For the first time, the LGBTQ rights movement garnered substantial support from outside of the LGBTQ community. These supporters, which have been critiqued for being primarily white heterosexual cisgender women, took on the cause of marriage equality and devoted time and resources toward the cause (see Chauncey 2009). However, after *Obergefell v. Hodges*, these same allies saw the work of the movement as done rather than just beginning. In truth, the contemporary LGBTQ rights movement has largely not been about marriage equality, as queer activism has broadened and refocused on social justice issues facing the community, including crucial conversations about transgender and intersex rights, intersections of identity (including race, HIV status, sex work, socioeconomics, homelessness, and much more), legal protection of gender identity, gender expression, sexuality, abolishing reparative therapy programs, and establishing a truly intersectional social justice movement.

The pride rainbow has developed substantial popularity among LGBTQ allies, and has been used in pride parades, ally groups, and throughout various campaigns for and celebrations of marriage equality. It has become the widely accepted symbol of the LGBTQ community and associated movements. The pink triangle, as an alternate symbol, has been largely untouched by ally movements, allowing it to retain its own distinct queerness. In some ways the pink triangle functions as an insider symbol, as it is unrecognized by many outside of the community. But, perhaps more importantly, it functions as a less-commodified symbol. The rainbow represents a different message than the pink triangle, as it is utilized a symbol of pride, with a message of "it gets better," and is symbolic of allyship. In a movement that can feel polluted by outside voices, the pink triangle, in contrast, is an edgier symbol, less about pride and more about challenging institutions of power and raising up the oppressed. Those embracing the pink triangle recognize that celebrations of LGBTQ pride still privilege white, male, cisgender, able-bodied, socioeconomically privileged individuals; and the pink triangle represents the oppressions still faced by the LGBTQ community, often ignored or masked by the celebrations of marriage equality or well-intentioned allies who do not experience the daily lived experiences of the queer community.

Third, folklore teaches others and reinforces cultural values, which can be seen in the pink triangle's representation of collective community values and the affirmation of varied identities. Although the idea of widespread LGBTQ pride is important, LGBTQ community identity and acceptance run deeper, pointing to a collective kinship of chosen family, one with its own culture, traditions, language, rites, and symbols. This is a powerful identity, especially for queer youth. LGBTQ youth face a staggeringly high risk of suicide and self-harm. Community identity, especially the idea of chosen community, sends a message of collective voice ("we will be your voice when you are silenced") and solidarity. As part of the coming out process, many LGBTQ youth go through phases of strongly identifying with the community or experiencing a sense of queer pride (Ali and Barden 2015; Dunlap 2014). Unlike other cultures that children inherit from their caregivers, LGBTQ youth most commonly enter the larger queer community without previous community fluency. As they learn the social and cultural norms of the community, folklore and symbols take on special meaning. The pink triangle is one of many symbols or cultural items that is transmitted as part of queer social structures and norms, reinforcing cultural fluency and community identity.

Finally, folklore functions as a means of social control. Typically this manifests folklorically in establishing morals, values, or means of defining community connectivity. In this case, the pink triangle delineates group affiliation. By using the symbol, individuals publicly mark their LGBTQ identity and fluency. The interesting twist is that non-LGBTQ individuals may also employ the pink triangle to indicate that they are allies or that they have undergone SafeZone training. Although not immediately a part of the community, these individuals use the symbol to exhibit that they are also aligned, at least philosophically or politically, with the LGBTQ community. In this way the pink triangle establishes who is in and who is, for lack of a better phrase, out, allowing for individuals to function as either full or partial insiders.

THE PINK TRIANGLE'S SUSTAINABILITY AS A SYMBOL

Clearly the pink triangle has significance for folklorists. But, in the end, why is the reinvigoration of the pink triangle significant for the queer community? Why are LGBTQ teens and young adults, who are unaware of their engagement with folklore, using the symbol with increased frequency? And is the pink triangle a sustainable symbol or will its popularity fade? There are four main reasons for the reinvigoration of the Rosa Winkel: the role of marriage equality in queer rights activism, conversations around bullying, symbol replication, and broad identity inclusion.

First, after same-sex marriage in the United States evolved into the "new" LGBTQ political cause, there has remained an interest in young LGBTQ adults to engage as queer rights activists. Unlike the rainbow, for young adults, the pink triangle harkens back to activism during the AIDS epidemic.

It is symbolic of a level of passionate engagement on behalf of the LGBTQ community that is once again on the rise. The ability to link their current activism to that of the forerunners of queer activism creates a feeling of shared legacy and community history; this includes the persecution of gay men during the Holocaust. A good example of the way the symbol has arched across generations is Leonard Matlovich's grave. The gravestone, located in Washington D.C.'s Congressional Cemetery, bears only his last name at the foot of the grave border. The headstone is inscribed with two pink triangles: one with the point down (inscribed: Never Again, 6 July 1943) and one with the point upward (inscribed: Never Forget, 22 June 1988). Below these triangles the epitaph reads, "A Gay Vietnam Veteran—When I was in the military they gave me a medal for killing two men and a discharge for loving one." Now a popular queer pilgrimage site, the grave which evokes the Rosa Winkel of the Holocaust and the pink triangle of 1980s LGBTQ activism bridges generations. In May 2011 veteran Captain Stephen Hill and Josh Snyder married in front of the stone, and their wedding pictures went viral in online communities of young LGBTQ adults.[3] The gravestone has also been the site of protests for the repeal of Don't Ask, Don't Tell, as well as Veteran's Day celebrations that honor LGBTQ veterans, especially those who were dishonorably discharged because of their sexuality or gender identity.

Second, in a culture where we are finally talking about the devastating impact of bullying, the voices of queer youth remain overwhelmingly silent in this conversation. The pink triangle empowers them by linking the hate that they are experiencing with a legacy of others who have also been targeted because of their sexuality or perceived differences. It is a powerful lesson to realize that they are not alone and that their voices matter. As an alternate symbol to the pride rainbow, the pink triangle offers a symbol that represents those who are not out, who are struggling with feeling a sense of pride, or who are looking for a symbol that represents their feelings of being counter-cultural, stealth, or different.

Third, on the most fundamental level, the pink triangle is easy to replicate. It lends itself well to being drawn, reproduced, and tattooed. It is easily incorporated into logos and, perhaps even more importantly, is easy for youth to draw on notebooks, with pens or markers on their bodies, to be created in an online forum, as amateur tattoo artists, or to use in printed literature. The ease of its reproduction significantly adds to the appeal of the pink triangle. A test of this will be whether the pink triangle continues to increase in popularity after the addition of the pride flag (2016) and the rainbow (2010) to the Unicode Standard List of emoji. The red triangle, used in text platforms as an alternate to the pink triangle, was added in 2010 and relaunched in 2015 with both the point facing downward (as is usually seen in Holocaust representations) and upward (usually used in queer reproductions). In online forums it is popular to use the rainbow when supporting the community and the pink triangle when speaking of the self or in attempts to remain "stealth" (not out) as a young LGBTQ adult.

Fourth, as the LGBTQ community expands to better represent an encompassing understanding of identities, the pink triangle feels "fresh." Despite the fact that it predates the pride rainbow, its reinvigoration makes it feel underground, young, and new. Although the rainbow remains enormously popular, the pink triangle has been rendered a new pride symbol for a younger generation. The rainbow, although encompassing in its representation of the community, does not have the same countercultural vibe that some LGBTQ youth seek. If the rainbow is the symbol of an older generation, the pink triangle is the symbol of a younger, digital generation. Although it has not eclipsed or surpassed the rainbow in usage, the pink triangle has found voice in younger queer spaces that have reclaimed the symbol for their use.

Will the pink triangle have staying power and continue to increase in popularity? It is difficult to say. It would seem most likely that its popularity will continue to ebb and flow. When I first began this study, I postured that the true test would be if the symbol remained popular after marriage equality became a national right in the United States. Now, several years after *Obergefell v. Hodges*, that seems shortsighted. (To be fair, my initial inquiries into the pink triangle came at a time when marriage equality felt like a distant dream). A truer test will be to monitor how this generation continues to engage the pink triangle, if it still resonates, or if they find themselves confronted by a new symbol set that better suits their needs. Perhaps the fact that the pink triangle has become a popular tattoo will increase its literal staying power.

Ultimately, the pink triangle has evolved from its stigmatizing Holocaust origins. Although these historic roots led to its resonance with the queer community during the AIDS crisis, contemporary understandings of the symbol has evolved away from Holocaust symbology. For the contemporary youth that use it, the pink triangle has little to do with the Holocaust; rather, it indicates a shared history, establishes who has community cultural fluency, denotes inclusion and acceptance, and represents the continuing fight for queer rights. In the end, it is not surprising that the pink triangle has regained popularity. It is a symbol of American LGBTQ youth finding their voice within the larger culture and within the queer community. The power of the symbol being recast should not be overlooked. Once worn by those stripped of their dignity and denied their voice, the Rosa Winkel now represents community pride and shared history. It speaks volumes, saying, "We were once victims, but no longer. As a community, we were, we are, and we will continue to be. It really does get better."

NOTES

1. I recognize the lack of treatment of lesbians and the trans community in this chapter. However, because of my focus on the pink triangle, I have limited my analysis to the gay male Holocaust experience and symbolic representation.

2. The closed group can be found here: https://www.facebook.com/groups/lgbts-againstmisuseofpinktriangle/.

3. The pink triangle is featured on other prominent graves, including Barbara Gittings and Kay Tobin Lahusen. Gittings is well known for her work to have the American Psychiatric Association change its policy that LGBTQ individuals were mentally ill. Lahusen, cofounder of Daughters of Bilitis, and author of *The Gay Crusaders*, was equally influential in early gay rights movements. The two are memorialized on a grave bench, featuring the pink triangle and inscribed "Gay pioneers who spoke truth to power: GAY IS GOOD." Similarly, Tom Swann's grave features the pink triangle in the center of an eagle, with the epitaph "Proud Gay Veteran: Never give up hope or give in to discrimination." Located near Matlovich's grave, Michael William Hildebrand's grave stone is shaped like a pyramid and is made of a reddish stone, a nod to the pink triangle, and is inscribed, "it was said of him that he had the gift to give love to those who felt unloved."

Chapter Five

Queerly Stitched

Religious Garb and LGBTQ Jewish Pride Symbols

On April 27, 2018, Hillel International posted a picture on Facebook of a college-aged woman smiling broadly. She was wearing a T-shirt with the outline of the state of Ohio that was filled in with rainbow stripes and had the word "pride" in white through the middle. The post was part of the woman's story, where she detailed how the Jewish communities of her childhood were not affirming of her identity but that through Hillel she was able to reconcile her sexuality with her love of Judaism. She goes on to explain how she helped establish "Nice Jewish Queers," an LGBTQ Jewish student group, as well as how the group has hosted queer *Seders*, LGBTQ *Shabbats*, and other community-building activities. Noticeably missing in the beautiful student portrait, though, is any symbol of Jewishness. If one were to have skipped reading the text, the image alone uses only LGBTQ symbols. It is only through the picture's caption that the reader learns the story of her queer Jewish identity. This is not meant to be a critique of the student, but rather a comment on how the symbol set afforded to this young woman does not allow her to adequately express her full story. The choice to externalize multiple identities is familiar in many contemporary discussions of intersectionality, but this chapter specifically probes the question of why the symbols take on significant meaning in social scripting when they are expressed on the body. This chapter begins by offering a brief overview of the history of LGBTQ acceptance in the Jewish community, followed by a detailed description of certain Jewish LGBTQ body practices and pride symbols. Ultimately it argues that, through the presentation of the self, queer Jewish symbology challenges the privatization of contemporary American culture in ways that shift the understanding of social scripts such that the body becomes the central text for navigating overlapping Jewish and LGBTQ identities.

JUDAISM AND LGBTQ ACCEPTANCE

Like most other religions, Judaism has historically been divided over issues of LGBTQ acceptance (Drinkwater 2016). Traditionally these views have been based on Leviticus 18:22 (you shall not lie with a male as with a woman; it is an abomination) and Leviticus 20:13 (if a man lies with a male as with a woman, both of them have committed an abomination; they shall be put to death; their blood is upon them). Torah scholars have wrestled with these two passages, arguing for and against the LGBTQ community. Most liberal interpretations view the texts to be speaking against Israelites copying religious practices from other nations, which is a theme throughout the larger text. In this interpretation, having sex with children or with temple prostitutes of either gender would be considered against Israelite religious practice. In essence, because the writers of the Torah could not conceptualize a committed LGBTQ couple or family, they are writing about abuses of power within sexual relationships and are not actually speaking against a consensual loving LGBTQ relationship (Guest 2006; Plaskow and Shneer 2009; Tabb Stewart 2017).

That interpretation of text has continued to evolve alongside secular American LGBTQ acceptance. At first, the text was used to condemn sexual acts and not individuals; in other words, as long as an LGBTQ person (as the text was interpreted to include the entire queer community and not just gay men) remained celibate, he or she was not breaking *halakhic* directive. Later, as secular society increasingly accepted the LGBTQ community, movement was made within the Conservative, Reconstructionist, and Reform movements to voice greater acceptance of queer Jews (Greenberg 2004; Kahn 1989; Schnoor 2006).[1]

Within mainstream non-Orthodox Judaism (Conservative, Reconstructionist, and Reform), LGBTQ acceptance began at the civil level and progressed to religious equality. One benchmark of LGBTQ religious acceptance is the ordination of openly queer clergy. In 1984, the Reconstructionist Rabbinical College became the first major rabbinical seminary to accept openly gay students. This was followed in 1990 by the Reconstructionist Rabbinical Assembly passing a resolution that established a non-discrimination policy in the placement of rabbinical jobs (Alpert, Elwell, and Idelson 2001).

After the Reform movement's 1977 resolution to end civil discrimination against the LGBTQ community, the Central Conference of American Rabbis (CCAR) established a Committee on Homosexuality and the Rabbinate in 1986, which created a report stating that "all rabbis, regardless of sexual orientation, be accorded the opportunity to fulfill the sacred vocation that they have chosen." In 1990, CCAR endorsed the report and changed the admissions policy of their rabbinical seminary, Hebrew Union College-Jewish Institute of Religion (HUC-JIR) (CCAR 2015).

The Conservative movement considered the ordination of LGBTQ clergy in 1992, but on March 25, 1992, the Committee on Jewish Law and Standards (CLJS) voted against ordaining gay clergy and issued a Consensus Statement on Homosexuality. This statement detailed how the Conservative movement would not admit openly LGBTQ individuals into rabbinical or cantorial schools. The statement did not include a "ruling" on whether or not openly queer Jews could serve in other leadership roles within the Jewish community and ended with a hint of ambiguity, saying, "gays and lesbians are welcome in our congregations, youth groups, camps, and schools." In 2002, the CLJS revisited these questions and in 2006 accepted position papers both suggesting change and adhering to tradition. In doing so, they attempted to create a middle ground, allowing rabbis, synagogues, and other religious institutions to decide whether or not they want to perform same-sex weddings or hire openly LGBTQ clergy. Just as not all Conservative synagogues are egalitarian or will have a female rabbi, not all Conservative temples are affirming of the LGBTQ community. Framed as "struggling with multiple truths," this compromise solution is both progress (as openly gay students can now apply for admission to both American-based Conservative seminaries) and regression (as one of the opinion papers supported reparative therapy as a potential resource for LGBTQ Jews, and the paper that allowed for same-sex marriage and LGBTQ ordination still prohibits male anal sex) (Krawitz 2004; Solomon 2017).

Orthodox Judaism continues to reject same-sex relationships, believing that they are fundamentally against Jewish law. However, there seems to be some movement toward greater tolerance (which is in contrast to inclusion and integration); in 2010 over 200 Orthodox rabbis signed a statement that expressly welcomed gay Jews into synagogues (although the statement still reiterated Orthodoxy's stance against LGBTQ acceptance). Grassroots groups like JQY and Eshel continue to work for change and greater LGBTQ acceptance within the Orthodox community (Ariel 2007; Halbertal and Koren 2006; Itzhaky and Kissil 2015; Mark 2008; Rapoport 2004).

But what does any of this mean for Jews in practice? Like much of secular discourse around LGBTQ rights, attention tends to focus on marriage and other civil rights. Among the mainstream Jewish movements, all non-Orthodox denominations perform same-sex marriage ceremonies. Reform and Reconstructionist rabbis consider same-sex marriages to qualify as *kiddushin* (a holy union between two partners), while Conservative rabbis do not refer to it as such (nor are they required to perform these ceremonies). Certainly civil rights are of importance for LGBTQ Jews, but true inclusion into Jewish life necessitates greater acceptance and integration—and recognition that gender nonconforming, nonbinary, and trans identified Jews have largely been overlooked in discussions of queer Judaism.

At the forefront of LGBTQ Jewish inclusion is Keshet, a cross-denominational organization that works "for a world in which all Jewish organizations and communities are strengthened by LGBTQ inclusive policy, programming, culture, and leadership and where Jews of all sexual orientations and gender identities can live fully integrated Jewish lives" (Keshet n.d.). Keshet supports queer Jewish life through a number of initiatives, including leadership education, community-building initiatives, safe space programs, parent education and mobilization to support LGBTQ children, advocating for policy reform, and in the development of a vast array of resources for individuals, families, synagogues, community leaders, and schools.[2]

LGBTQ JEWISH GARB AND FASHION

As a folklorist interested in collecting and analyzing LGBTQ Jewish material culture and bodylore, I have identified five primary categories of LGBTQ Jewish items: items which can be worn (*tallitot, tefillin, kippot,* T-shirts, jewelry and pins, tattoos,[3] etc.); foodstuffs (rainbow *challah,* rainbow *hamentashen* [cookies eaten at Purim], the orange on the *Seder* plate); items which can be used or displayed (rainbow *menorahs* [candelabras], rainbow *mezuzzot* [a case holding scripture on a doorway], rainbow *Shabbat* candlesticks, flags, stained glass, art, cross-stitch, mugs, etc.); symbols or signs used to identify spaces or groups (brochures, signage, safe space demarcation, media representation, protest signs, etc.); and novelty items (gay Moses dolls, humorous pins, plastic rainbow bracelets, rainbow Star of David toys, stickers, bumper stickers, etc.). This list does not include a rhetorical analysis of liturgy (including naming ceremonies and marriage ceremonies), although these linguistic shifts are also important, but rather material items that can be created, purchased, or otherwise consumed. Likewise, it does not address issues of access to space, from the *mikveh* and the Western Wall, especially for trans Jews or nonbinary Jews. All of these issues warrant study, but for the purposes of this chapter, I focus on items that can be worn on the body as distinct from items that can be displayed or consumed separately from the body, and include a description of *yarmulkes, tallisim, tefillin,* T-shirts, and pins and jewelry.

Yarmulkes

One of the first items of Jewish garb to be "modified" as an LGBTQ pride item was the *kippah/yarmulke.* As the most easily stylized form of Jewish religious garb, it is an item that is already highly personalized. Variations in *yarmulkes* range from favorite sports teams to solid color designs. Available in a wide variety of fabrics, sizes, and even shapes (including the traditional skullcap design and the more hat-like bucharian *kippah*), *yarmulkes* can be hand embroidered, crocheted, inscribed with dates and names, or otherwise adorned (Baizerman 1992; Davis and Davis 1983; Silverman 2012).

Unlike some other traditional forms of Jewish religious garb, the *yarmulke* is an item that is more likely to be handcrafted or designed. Because of this, it lends itself well to the creation of pride *yarmulkes* (see Milligan 2013; Milligan 2014b). These head coverings are typically rainbow colored and come in numerous designs. For example, some are constructed using pie-shaped pieces in each color of the rainbow, creating a circular color-blocked design. Crocheted *yarmulkes*, often in the *kippah sruga* style (associated with Religious Zionism), utilize variegated yarn to create an interlocking rainbow appearance. More advanced fiber artists have created color-blocked *yarmulkes*, as well as *yarmulkes* that have a rainbow border against a solid center. Other pride *yarmulkes* have been created using printed fabric (especially bucharian *kippot*), painting on leather, tie-dying, or by adorning *yarmulkes* with piping, puff paint, embroidery, or other forms of craft personalization.

Steeped in traditionalism and maleness, the use of *yarmulkes* by women or others perceived as "on the margins" of Judaism has been problematized by scholars, who question the motivations behind wearing the symbol (Darwin 2017; Darwin 2018; Milligan 2013, 2014a, 2014b). Two primary trends emerge: some marginalized Jews wear the symbol as part of their own Jewish religious practice and others wear *yarmulkes* as a feminist or political statement. In this frame, regardless of her intent, the marginalized body wearing a *yarmulke* is politically suspect in ways that a heterosexual cisgender man is not, as her audience assumes her intent rather than accepting it as part of her public performance of Jewishness.

Tallisim

The *tallis* a Jewish prayer shawl. Traditionally a large rectangle of fabric, the *tallis* can be made from wool, cotton, or synthetic fibers. Some contemporary *tallisim* are smaller and similar to long scarves. At the four corners of the *tallis* are *tzitzit*, strings that are tied in a specific pattern. The *tallis* is worn during worship and prayer, and, like most of Jewish garb, it is traditionally only worn by men. In contemporary practice, *tallisim* are worn by both men and women in non-Orthodox denominations, but they are not as common as *yarmulkes* (see Silverman 2012).

Like *yarmulkes*, *tallisim* can also be stylized in fabric, color, and design. However, *tallisim* are significantly more expensive and less commodified than *yarmulkes*, meaning that an individual is less likely to own several or purchase "novelty" *tallisim*. Because of this, pride *tallisim* are particularly significant, as they indicate a substantial investment in the prayer shawl, suggesting a greater commitment to owning and wearing LGBTQ Jewish religious garb.

The most familiar rainbow *tallis* was designed by Rabbi Zalman Schachter-Shalomi, known as Reb Zalman by his followers, and is popular both in the Renewal movement and in other non-Orthodox communities. His design is interchangeably called the *B'nai Or* (children of light) *tallis*,[4] Joseph's Coat (although Reb Zalman never called it this himself), or the Reb Zalman rainbow *tallis*.

Even for those unfamiliar with the name, the design is recognizable. The *tallis* is (usually) white with black and rainbow stripes and is the traditional large rectangular shape. The first *B'nai Or tallis* was made in the 1950s after Reb Zalman had a revelation during meditation. He was meditating on the *midrash* "How did God create the world? God wrapped Godself in a robe of light and it began to shine," and was overcome with the image of a vibrant rainbow prayer shawl. He considered several initial designs, trying to retain both a traditional *tallis* design while also embracing a spectrum of color. At first he tried embroidering a traditional *tallis* and later also tried applying appliquéd stripes.

Ultimately, Reb Zalman decided that he wanted to have the rainbow of colors actually woven into the fabric, in the same construction that other Orthodox prayer shawls are made. He struggled to find a weaver to make what some dismissively referred to as his "clown *tallis*." Ultimately, he contracted with Vetements Riligieux, a Christian vestment company in Montreal, Canada, to create five rainbow *tallisim*. He kept one for himself and gave away the others to Abraham Joshua Heschel, Everett Gendler, Arthur Green, and an unidentified fifth person (Gershom n.d.).

Reb Zalman's original design was based in kabbalistic inspiration, but regardless of his original intent, the integration of the rainbow has rendered his *tallis* a Jewish pride symbol.[5] Outside of the Renewal movement, the *B'nai Or tallis* is interpreted differently depending on context. In other non-orthodox communities, the rainbow *tallis* can be read as an indicator of someone's affiliation with the Renewal movement, as an LGBTQ pride symbol, or as a nod to Joseph's coat of many colors or to Noah's Ark (i.e., someone's personal connection to a story or a stylistic choice for a particular motif).

Rainbow *tallisim* are not limited to the *B'nai Or* design. Other designs eliminate the black stripes; some broaden or narrow the size of the stripes, placing them at different intervals; some use ribbon or satin appliqués on top of a woven *tallis*; others use embroidery to achieve intricate rainbow designs;

some are abstract in their interpretation of the rainbow, using color blocking or various shapes instead of traditional stripes; finally, some integrate words (shalom, pride, love, peace) or images (hearts, peace signs, rainbow pomegranates, rainbows with clouds).

The stylization of *tallisim* also includes the *atarah* and the *tallis* bag. The *atarah*, literally the crown, refers to the collar of the *tallis*. It is typically embroidered in gold or silver thread. Some rainbow *tallisim* use this as an additional space for using multicolored thread; others utilize it as the only rainbow space on the *tallis*, leaving the rest in a traditional design but customizing the *atarah* with rainbow colors. This type of customization is also seen with the *tallis* bag. Although the bag is not religious garb, its intimate association with the *tallis* renders it an extension of the garment. Typically, the bag matches the *tallis*, featuring the Hebrew word "*tallit*" across the front. The bag is a good indicator of whether the rainbow *tallis* is meant to symbolize Joseph's coat or Noah and the flood, because if association with those stories is the intention, the images typically appear on the bag even if they are not present on the *tallis*. Similarly, others who have pride *tallisim* also have a rainbow *tallis* bag, often with a stylized rainbow Star of David.

Tefillin

Tefillin, also known as phylacteries, are small leather boxes containing parchment inscribed with verses from the Torah. These boxes are wrapped around the forehead and the non-dominant arm and hand and are worn during morning services or prayer except on *Shabbat* or holidays. This practice evolved out of commandments in the Torah[6] and have subsequently been interpreted by the *Talmud* (a central Jewish text) with instruction on how the actual *tefillin* should be made and then bound to the body (Amit 2008; Cohn 2008; Silverman 2012). Most commonly, *tefillin* are worn by men in Orthodox and in some Conservative communities, although Jews across all denominations engage with the practice. Orthodox women do not lay *tefillin* (see Alexander 2011), and although women laying *tefillin* is uncommon, it is not prohibited in non-Orthodox communities.

In order for *tefillin* to be kosher, they must follow specific rules, including being made from a single piece of animal hide, having a base with an upper compartment, and being inscribed with the Hebrew letter *shin* on the head-*tefillin*, so that when the straps are bound in a particular way it forms the Hebrew letters *shin, dalet, yud,* spelling *Shaddai*, one of the names of God. Four handwritten parchment scrolls inscribed with biblical passages are placed inside the boxes (Ehrman 2000; Greene 1992).[7]

It is extremely rare to see significant variations in *tefillin* stylization, as they are usually made of standardized black leather, although some natural variations do occur based on the quality of leather and the ways in which the leather is finished. Still, some *tefillin* have been modified to create pride *tefillin*. This is done in four primary ways: through wrapping embroidery thread around the leather, creating a non-permanent wrapping similar to how friendship bracelets are crafted; through embroidery of the leather; by painting or using paint pens to mark the leather; or by dying the leather. For those who regularly lay *tefillin*, the altering of the leather in this way holds a certain shock value. *Halakha* dictates that *tefillin* should have an outer surface that is black but that the underside can be any color except red as this is considered "disrespectful" because it could be mistaken for blood coming from the scabs of the wearer.[8] I have not been able to locate commentary addressing personalization or stylization of *tefillin*, suggesting that this practice is so uncommon that it has not drawn significant attention especially from Orthodox commentators. Furthermore, the *halakhic* validity of altered *tefillin* is likely not of importance for those who have stylized the leather in these ways.[9]

T-shirts

Although T-shirts are not religious garb, when religious symbols are used in their design, they engage overlapping symbol sets. LGBTQ Jewish T-shirt designs incorporate two primary motifs: using the rainbow on Jewish symbols or, less commonly, integrating Hebrew into more popular LGBTQ designs. As was discussed in chapter five, the pink triangle is a problematic symbol for many LGBTQ Jews, although it is one that is commonly used in queer spaces. Generally, T-shirts do not use the pink triangle in Jewish designs; instead, they utilize rainbow Stars of David, overlap Lambdas in rainbow colors to create the Star of David, or take a rainbow background and place a white or black Star of David on it. Other designs use an arched rainbow with a Star of David overlay, the Hebrew word "Shalom" written in rainbow colors, or the rainbow *hamsa* (a palm shaped amulet to protect against the evil eye).

Some novelty T-shirts reinterpret familiar designs, including "I (heart) NY" reprinted with "I (heart) Nice Jewish Boys" or "I (heart) Nice Jewish Girls." Another design takes the "Gay is OK" iconic block print and replaces the "O" with a Star of David. Similarly, the Human Rights Campaign has a popular T-shirt design that says "Love Conquers Hate," which is now available in a number of languages, including Hebrew. Finally, a few examples of inventive designs include "Oy Vey, I'm Gay," "Proud, Gay, and Jewish," "100% Gay & 100% Kosher," "Homophobia is an Abomination," "Fagele,"

"You're a Rainbow Bagel in a World Full of Everythings," and rainbows surrounded by unicorns and floating Stars of David. Also recently popular are depictions of a "Jewnicorn," a Jewish unicorn leaping over a rainbow.

Jewelry and Pins

Similar to T-shirts, jewelry is not regulated in the same way as religious garb, leaving ample space for creativity and design. Examples include rainbow Star of David necklace charms, Star of David charms with the equal symbol in the middle, rainbow beading with Jewish charms, Hebrew wedding rings with rainbow inlays, rainbow fabric chokers with Jewish charms, dog tags with the rainbow Star of David, and various plastic, leather, and canvas bracelets in rainbow colors with Jewish words (especially Shalom) or symbols (usually the Star of David or the *hamsa*). The rainbow typically features in either the arms of the Star of David (each of the six lines being a different color) or in the middle of the Star. Other Stars of David are created by overlaying a rainbow triangle with a white, black, or clear triangle. Similar designs are also found on earrings.

There are two primary types of pins that feature LGBTQ Jewish symbols. The first is lapel pins, which are either worn as adornment or on ties. These pins typically are streamlined in their appearance, as they are meant to be worn in more formal or business contexts, and feature the Star of David with some form of the rainbow, either as its center or in the color of the arms. Novelty pins, however, are much less regulated. They feature pithy sayings, much like the T-shirts described, or other identity descriptors like "Proud to be a Jewish Lesbian Feminist," "Jewish Dyke," and "Gay and Jewish AF."[10]

ANALYSIS: SOCIAL SCRIPTS
AND QUEER JEWISH SYMBOLOGY

The wearing of pride items or LGBTQ identifiers in Jewish spaces can be read a number of different ways. Traditionally academics, including myself, have utilized two general approaches. Some argue that Jewish LGBTQ symbols represent a statement of agency, a way of claiming space, a way of raising awareness, and at times a deliberate subversion of the anticipated "norm" (Alpert 1998; Brettschneider 2003; Duberman 1990; Jakobson 2003; Milligan 2014b). Others have approached these items as a portrayal of intersecting identities, a manifestation of a person made of many parts, and a way of externalizing the internal in recognizable and meaningful ways both for the individual and for her audience (Balka and Rose 1991; Brown 2004;

Cohen, Aviv, and Kelman 2009; Milligan 2013). Neither of these approaches is wrong, as they both point to a partial reality of embodying multiple identities. However, both approaches rely heavily on the perception of symbols; this generates a symbolic analysis that relies on the interpretation of an audience that, more than likely, does not share the same overlapping identities as the individual utilizing the Jewish LGBTQ symbol on her body. This type of interaction with symbols is in line with Erving Goffman's work on the performance of self (1959), but contemporary analysis has applied his framework to the intersectionalism[11] of the self that is portrayed by the individual utilizing the symbol. If LGBTQ culture is taught in queer spaces, and Jewish culture is taught in Jewish spaces, what does this mean for those who need to learn how to be an LGBTQ Jew? How is LGBTQ Jewish space defined and what role does the body have in this definition?

Social scripts are part psychological behavioristic analysis. These scripts relate to the societal and cultural expectations of individuals and their interactions with one another (Goffman 1959; Pelligrini 1997). Individuals learn these scripts through habit, practice, routine, and peer regulation (Ponse 1978; Rosario, Schrimshaw, and Hunter 2008). These scripts play out in dramaturgy, which is the Erving Goffman's sociological theory of how daily social interactions are scripted (1959). This theatrical metaphor for life has the actor present herself to the audience in ways that are steeped in cultural norms and beliefs. In turn, the audience understands the individual based on both the actor's performance and their own preconceived notions and experiences. On the front or main stage, the actor is expected to behave a certain way so that the audience will accept her performance. Backstage, the actor can drop her mask, allowing herself to step out of character and be her true self.

Goffman's front- and backstage dynamic posits individuals as strangers who must learn from one another through their performances. LGBTQ Jewish symbols take on special significance, then, in the role of identity enactment. The creation of an LGBTQ symbol set is particularly significant because it blends two "paradoxical" identities, or at least two identities that traditionally have been at odds with one another, to create a collective identity for a group that does not exist separately from the two identities. On the front of stage, then, is the queer Jew, performing her role as both Jewish and LGBTQ for an audience that may only understand half of her performance. If Judaism is an ethno-religious identity that encompasses cultural and religious norms, and queerness is a social and cultural category, how does one blend the two in ways that allow the individual to be fully realized by both groups? Furthermore, without the creation of separate queer Jewish spaces, how does one learn the social script for being Jewishly queer and queerly Jewish?

As is detailed in chapter 4's discussion of the pink triangle, the LGBTQ community has struggled to identify around central symbols, as the community is defined primarily by its "otherness" in relation to sexuality and gender identity. By utilizing symbols like the rainbow and the pink triangle, the LGBTQ community establishes a shared history, creating a canon of collective experience growing out of the Holocaust and the AIDS epidemic. These symbols, also including the lambda, are conceptualized broadly such that they can encompass a wide range of sexuality and gender identities.

For Jews, shared universal symbols are also difficult. There is a rich tradition of Jewish symbology, including numerology, but the most universal icon of Judaism is the Star of David. Other symbols, like the *menorah*, the *shofar*, the letter *shin*, the lion of Judah, the stone tablets, and the *hamsa*, are familiar to those within the community but not recognizable to outsiders. This leaves LGBTQ Jews with relatively few combinations of symbols that are familiar to both of their audiences, especially when one recognizes that the use of Holocaust symbols, like the pink triangle, can be problematic for many Jews.

At first glance, it would seem that combining the rainbow with the Star of David is an easy solution, and in many cases it has been. However, turmoil erupted at the 2017 Chicago Dyke March over the use of a rainbow flag with a Star of David overlay. Three women were carrying these flags and were removed from the march when organizers indicated that the flags were "triggers" that could "inadvertently or advertently express Zionism" (Weiss 2017). Responses to this action came swiftly from both sides. Some agreed with the march organizers: the flags looked like the Israeli flag, which also has a Star of David in the center, and therefore were symbols of Zionist oppression. Others were in direct opposition, pointing out anti-Semitism, and articulating that queer Jews were left with no viable symbols if the rainbow Star of David is taken from them—and also astutely noting that the Star of David does not necessarily indicate Zionism or support for Israel any more than it supports the Holocaust, although the symbol was also used by Nazis to mark Jews. In a *New York Times* piece by Bari Weiss discussing the event (2017), she asks progressive American Jews, "Which side of your identity do you keep, and which side do you discard and revile? Do you side with the oppressed or with the oppressor?"

Not only must LGBTQ Jews struggle to claim ownership of overlapping symbols, like the rainbow Star of David flag, but their bodies also become a source of potential politicization. Both Jewish identity and LGBTQ identity are scripted on the body by outside culture. Jews, as detailed in chapter 1, have a long history of being considered corporally different (Edelman 2000; Gilman 1991), including anti-Semitic beliefs of genetic inferiority to stereotypes of menstruating men, big noses, curly hair, flat feet, and overall weakness. Spiritual and religious belief takes secondary importance in the consideration of the Jewish body, as it is racialized regardless of religious practice. This type of embodied politic is also present in the LGBTQ community. LGBTQ identity is far more than sexual practice and gender expression, but outsiders often characterize and misunderstand the LGBTQ community in ways that reduce queerness to stereotypes.[12]

If the body is politicized by the audience in ways that the performer does not control, the enacted script of LGBTQ Jewish performance is fraught with anxieties before the performer even enters the stage. In line with Richard Sennett's work (1977), in which he identifies the limitations of community and public spaces, one of the tensions of contemporary identity is the relative unfamiliarity individuals have with one another. In other words, one of the challenges of modern life is that individuals are strangers to one another, establishing insecurities that motivate displays of identity in order to foster the navigation of social scripts. For Sennett, the ways in which people dress, their gestures, and other performance of self all become methods of engaging others, especially strangers. These actions allow individuals to create social bonds and to navigate public interactions. In shared spaces, which hold the potential for discomfort or awkward interactions because of an increasingly privatized culture, engaging symbology enables individuals to culturally encode themselves and enact a social script of the body. In other words, the private behavior of an LGBTQ Jew is not contested, but her public performance is a signal both to her audience and to herself of her belonging and fluency in the social behavioral script of *both* groups.

When Sennett's theory of interpersonal unfamiliarity is applied in the specific case of LGBTQ Jews, it manifests in three ways: in the Jewish space, in the LGBTQ space, and ultimately in the intersection which forms the lived experience of the individual. In other words, Jewish spaces do not possess the scripts necessary for adequately recognizing and supporting LGBTQ Jews. Parallelly, LGBTQ spaces have not developed the cultural scripts for integrating and acknowledging queer Jewishness. The LGBTQ Jew, then, is forced to navigate public and personal life, including Jewish and queer spaces, without an established and accepted social script that recognizes her overlapping identities. The scripting of Jewishness is taught in the family, in the synagogue, or in the religious and cultural community. The scripting of queerness is taught in personal interactions, LGBTQ spaces, and, more recently, online. And, while it is true that fluency in queer culture is often learned as an adult, the transmission process is increasingly less underground and more accessible to younger individuals.

With the privatization of American culture, the self emerges as the most familiar space. When entering into potentially unfamiliar or unscripted spaces, the individual can rely on the body as the central locus of the familiar. By externalizing both Jewishness and queerness, the individual creates a secure public space for herself. Similar to the body engagement of women in the Renewal movement described in chapter 2, the body becomes how LGBTQ Jews do queerness Jewishly and Judaism queerly.

The notable exception is the LGBTQ synagogue. These temples, including Beth Chayim Chadashim (Los Angeles), Sha-ar Zahav (San Francisco), Beit Simchat Torah (New York City), Bet Mishpachah (Washington, D.C.), and Beth Ahavah (Philadelphia), are explicitly queer Jewish synagogues. In these spaces, which might also be expanded to include events sponsored by Keshet, there is an anticipated social fluency in both Jewishness and queerness. And yet these congregations are shifting, as can be seen in San Francisco's Congregation Sha-ar Zahav announcing that it was "de-emphasizing" itself as a queer synagogue, paralleled by New York City's Beit Simchat Torah identifying itself as an LGBTQS synagogue. (The "S" stands for "straight.") Although both synagogues maintain that they centralize queer social values in their Jewish spaces, they identify struggling because most LGBTQ Jews are not interested in synagogue life. Similarly, they articulate experiencing that LGBTQ Jews who are interested in congregational affiliation tend to increasingly join mainstream temples, especially as there has been nationally increased acceptance of the LGBTQ community (Gloster 2017; see Shokeid 1995).

Just as LGBTQ synagogues are reimagining themselves and the orange on the *Seder* plate has been recast to represent identities beyond the LGBTQ community, will queer Jewish garb and fashion become redundant with time? It would seem unlikely that that day will be soon, but that one can expect these symbols to continue evolving along with the communities that they represent. Other Jewish body practices and body rituals have not expanded to fully encompass the LGBTQ community, particularly to meet the needs of trans identified, nonbinary, and gender nonconforming Jews.[13] With the hope for eventual change in these rituals, surely these symbols will take on new meaning or form. Likewise, with a resurgence in American tattoo culture, it seems likely that these symbols will find new manifestations of literal embodiment that might replace the more transient use of religious garb as an expression of integrated personhood.

Because of the invisibility of the queer Jew (especially in worship space), these symbols are increasingly important. "Allyship" has diluted the efficacy of many LGBTQ Jewish symbols. Queer Jews grapple with the tensions created when esoteric symbols (either of coded identity or of stigmatization) enter the trendy vernacular. In other words, when synagogues post about pride events and non-LGBTQ Jews wear marriage equality pins, do queer Jewish symbols retain their worth? Moreover, is the synagogue necessarily a safe place for LGBTQ congregants?

With the commodification and acceptance of certain pride symbols into the general cultural vernacular, for example the equality symbol or the rainbow pride bracelet, queer Jewish religious garb takes on special significance. The overlap of religious garb and LGBTQ Jewish symbols is important because of the space it creates on the body for individuals to represent their overlapping identities. By engaging symbols that speak to both Jewishness and queerness, the embodied text sends a message to the audience (we are here), fellow actors (we might be the same), and the self (I am fully embodied in my identity).

This type of symbology takes two private identities, ethno-religious and sexuality/gender identity, and publicizes them using symbols that may or may not be recognized by others. In queer spaces, LGBTQ Jewish symbols generally do not include religious garb (*tallisim, kippot, tefillin*) because the "stage" is not an appropriate scene for these items. Therefore, jewelry, pins, and T-shirts are more likely to be used. In sacred spaces, though, religious garb and the integration of LGBTQ Jewish symbols take on special significance in their reflection of encompassing personhood.

In the end, does it actually matter if the audience recognizes these symbols? I would argue that it does not, because the significance of the symbols is in their *potential* for recognition and in the self-recognition experienced by the individual. In a time of public disconnect and privatization, LGBTQ Jewish symbols open the door for connecting to others in meaningful ways. And even if they go unrecognized, there is deep personal satisfaction of embodying overlapping identities fully, knowing that one appears before her audience engaging a symbolic script in ways that ensure that she is no longer invisible.

NOTES

1. It is worth noting that the Renewal movement has long voiced acceptance of LGBTQ Jews, as it is actually one of the hallmarks of movement.

2. For more on Keshet and their important work, visit their website at: https://www.keshetonline.org.

3. LGBTQ Jewishly themed tattoos include rainbow Stars of David, rainbow *hamsas*, Holocaust tattoos (especially those that include the pink triangle, as discussed in chapter 4), and rainbow stylized COEXIST and RESPECT tattoos (in which each of the letters is a religious or peace symbol). Others use Hebrew words or biblical text, often from the Song of Songs, written in rainbow ink or stylized with rainbow motifs around them. I mention tattoos here because I classify them as part of embodied queer Jewish folklore. However, I do not discuss them in depth in this chapter because of

its concentration on garb, which does not have the same permanence as tattoos. Still, both are important demonstrations of forms of queer Jewish embodiment.

4. *B'nai Or* is the original name of the group Reb Zalman led which broke from traditional denominational Judaism, now commonly referred to as the Renewal Movement.

5. To be fair, a pride symbol in Renewal contexts is in line with the movement's radically progressive integration and celebration of LGBTQ Jews.

6. Deuteronomy 11:18, Exodus 13:9, Exodus 13:16, and Deuteronomy 6:9.

7. These texts include Exodus 13:1–10, Exodus 13:11–16, Deuteronomy 6:3–9, and Deuteronomy 11:13–21.

8. Schulchan Arukh 33:4.

9. I had initially suspected that I might find some commentary or applications on the crossover of the leather of the *tefillin* with the LGBTQ leather community. In personal conversation, this has been referenced, but I have been unable to find any concrete mentions of it in scholarly or Jewish written works. This is also true for leather *kippot*.

10. "AF" is a colloquial abbreviation for "as fuck."

11. As someone working at the crossroads of two identities, I have labeled my work intersectional, but have come to recognize that "intersectionality" has been used so much in recent analysis that it has been diluted. Sumi Cho, Kimberlé Williams Crenshaw, and Leslie McCall note that when black feminists first introduced intersectionality in the late 1980s, it was intended to "focus attention on the vexed dynamics of difference and the solidarities of sameness in the context of antidiscrimination and social movement politics" (2013, 786). Contemporary usage of the term and theoretical framework has diverged from these roots, employing intersectionality to discuss overlapping identities and not to address underlying social power dynamics. As Cho, Crenshaw, and McCall note, "intersectionality is inextricably linked to an analysis of power, yet one challenge to intersectionality is its alleged emphasis on categories of identity versus structures of inequality" (ibid., 797). They critique how the framework has moved away from its initial analysis of power and exclusion and is being used by scholars to broadly consider overlapping identities. In other words, true studies of intersectionality are investigations of the structures that value or devalue individuals based on their identities, in contrast to inquiries that consider how an individual amalgamates her own overlapping identities. The crossroads of difference and identity demand contextualization and cultural situation. Taking heed of Cho, Crenshaw, and McCall's critique, traditionally the analysis of the overlapping identities of LGBTQ Jews has fallen squarely into the category of "intersectional" identity analysis that they critique. Most studies, including my own, have focused on how LGBTQ Jews work to navigate their dual identities as queer Jews, both in Jewish and in queer spaces (Abes 2011; Balka and Rose 1991; Barrow and Kuvalanka 2011; Boyarin, Itzkovitz, and Pelligrini 2003; Brown 2004; Cohen, Aviv, and Kelman 2009; Duberman 1990; Milligan 2013; Milligan 2014b; Schimel 2002; Schnoor 2006). While some scholars have been attuned to what this means in terms of religious power dynamics (Alpert 1998; Balka and Rose 1991; Faulkner and Hecht 2010, Krawitz

2004; Shneer and Aviv 2002), the focus on overlapping identities has not taken a truly intersectional approach.

12. Some forms of queer body stereotypes include the effeminate gay man, the butch lesbian, the promiscuous bisexual, and the societal pressures of "passing" on the trans and gender nonconforming community.

13. The Jewish community, much like American society at large, is finally coming to terms with the fact that they have overlooked the experiences and needs of transgender and nonbinary identifying people. Acceptance and support of trans Jews has followed a similar trajectory to LGB Jews. The first Reform transgender rabbi was ordained in 2006, and the most current (2007) *siddur* includes specific blessings for gender transition. A statement was released by the CCAR in 2015 that explicitly calls for full equality and inclusion for transgender individuals. The Conservative movement has taken a middle-of-the-road approach, releasing an opinion paper in 2003 that endorsed full sex reassignment surgery as necessary for an official sex change within Jewish law. (Those who have not undergone surgery or elected to have only partial gender affirming surgery are not considered, under this *halakhic* interpretation, to have transitioned within Conservative interpretation of Jewish law.) Within Orthodoxy, gender affirming surgeries, "cross-dressing," and hormone treatments are forbidden, although some progress has been made in terms of Orthodox discussions of welcoming transgender congregants.

Conclusion

Applications of Jewish Feminist Bodylore

Recently, in the midst of writing this book, I received an anti-Semitic email; the letter was pages upon pages of single spaced vitriol. I read it carefully out of morbid curiosity. The message's content was angry, uninformed, and rested on the very stereotypes of the Jewish body described in chapter 1. The writer briefly covered common anti-Semitic accusations including controlling banks and the media, but he spent the majority of his text pontificating on the genetic inferiority of Jews. He wrote, "Only one race of people have [*sic*] curly hair . . . and only one minority have [*sic*] Tasacks [*sic*] . . . and believe it or not there is [*sic*] a sizable number of people who are born with long tails and hoved [*sic*] feet." He goes on to refer consistently to the "Negroid people called the Jews" and makes his white supremacists beliefs clear: he hates anyone who isn't white—including Jews.

As I talked about this email with colleagues, it became clear that there were two general responses. My Christian colleagues were horrified and shocked; they talked about how they had no idea that anti-Semitism like this still existed, and they expressed disbelief and unfamiliarity with some of the stereotypes the writer had used. My Jewish colleagues approached the message with a dark sense of humor and a healthy dose of caution; we joked about how no one with hooves could have typed something as lengthy as that vitriolic smut, but underneath the self-deprecating jokes, there was a knowing acknowledgment that this kind of hate is still very real, that this is the reason why we pray under armed guard on Friday nights, and that Jewish bodies are still stigmatized and marginalized.

I share this anecdote because it was a full circle moment for me. As I have written these chapters and considered innovative and exciting ways that the Jewish body is being reconceptualized and re-embodied by Jews, I have had colleagues challenge me to consider if we had, indeed, started to move beyond some of the historic anti-Semitic stereotypes of the Jewish body. But the answer is no—these stereotypes are still alive and pervasive. Yet, at the same time, the Jewish body is neither stagnant nor determined by anti-Semitism. Instead, the bodies of Jews continue to be defined from within rather than from without, by Jews engaging their bodies in meaningful ways despite outside definitions of the Jewish body.

Just as anti-Semitism is not dead, neither is feminism. I am troubled when I hear others say that we are in a post-feminist world. For many critics, feminism is a dirty word, a word that refers to angry man-hating women who are out for their own gain at the expense of men.[1] They believe that feminism is antiquated and done—that women have achieved full equality, that girl power is enough, and that women can "have it all." The face and causes of feminism may change with time, but the movement, methodologies, and theories are still of critical importance as long as gender, sex, and sexuality are being used as weapons in systems of power and oppression.

What does all of this mean for Jewish feminist bodylore? If the Jewish body remains contested, and if feminism is facing a lack of social recognition, does that mean that this type of work is trite? In fact, I would argue that the exact opposite is true. Because the Jewish body is contested and because feminism is reconceptualizing its tenets to be more sensitive to overlapping identities and privilege hierarchies (e.g., race, sexuality, gender identity, and socioeconomics), Jewish feminist bodylore is all the more important as a field of inquiry.

In the previous chapters, I have articulated a common methodological thread to demonstrate how a Jewish feminist bodylore methodology highlights the body in new and embodied ways. At its core, this methodology analyzes the ways in which culture and tradition are translated and communicated through the body, giving meaning both to the individual and to her audience. This distinction of individual and audience is important because it allows for symbols to function both privately and publicly and in both recognized and unrecognized ways. In the same way, it also allows symbols to have different meanings based on how they are perceived, regardless of the intention of the person utilizing the symbol.

This book has explored a number of different innovative Jewish body practices: subversive feminist bodies in the synagogue, women in the Renewal movement and their spiritual engagement with their bodies, mothers and daughters creating hair rituals, reconceptualizations of the pink triangle by LGBTQ young adults, and inventive Jewish pride symbols. At first glance, these practices may seem disparate. Indeed, the haircut of a small girl seems to have little in common with liturgical dance. However, each of these examples, as understood through the lens of feminist bodylore, addresses four central themes: a re-embodiment of the body, the potential for multiple interpretations of a symbol, a reconceptualization of the gendered Jewish body, and a space for the transmission of culture and community formation.

First, as described in chapter 2, Jewish practices have the potential for re-embodiment. This can manifest in a number of ways, but, in essence, this re-embodiment focuses on ways that the body can be interpreted, conceptualized, or "translated" such that it develops social or personal meaning. For the feminists described in chapter 1, this re-embodiment challenges the perception of their actions as subversive. Their presence on the *bimah* or in religious garb signals that they are laying claim to a tradition that is rightfully theirs. Their embodiment of Jewish practice reimagines Judaism for the next generation of girls, demonstrating that they can celebrate and articulate their bodies fully in synagogue life; that they can use symbols which have traditionally excluded women; and that this re-embodiment, although sometimes viewed as political by outsiders, is a celebration of personal spirituality and religious potential. This is the same potential demonstrated in feminist *upsherin* rituals. By taking a body practice like the first haircut and infusing it with Jewishness, these women demonstrate that they have a full toolkit of Jewish ritual from which they may choose. They use familiar Jewish body symbols—the haircut and the *alef-bet*—to create a meaningful rite of passage for their daughters. Likewise, by using symbols from the Jewish canon, including the word *upsherin*, the women legitimize their inventive practice and make it feel Jewish for participants.

These reimagined symbols are also present in the re-embodiment of the pink triangle and other queer Jewish symbology. For the young adults described in chapter 4 who engage the pink triangle as a positive symbol, they articulate a form of re-embodiment that reclaims and destigmatizes the physical plights experienced by both the victims of the Holocaust and the ravaged bodies of AIDS patients. In both cases, the literal wasting away of flesh and the destruction of the body is at the center of the narrative. By reclaiming the pink triangle as a shared and positive symbol of pride, young LGBTQ adults demonstrate a way of re-embodying not only historic bodies but also their own literal physical bodies, especially when they tattoo the symbol on themselves. The same is also true for LGBTQ Jewish pride symbols. By bringing pride symbols into Jewish spaces and by placing them on the physical body, they take on new meaning. Not only are the symbols meaningful for the individual who is wearing them, but they also demonstrate the need to have representations of Jewishness in LGBTQ spaces and of queerness in Jewish spaces. This re-embodiment is a statement of visibility.

Second, here also exists the potential for multiple interpretations of the symbols described. This is especially clear when considering how Jewish feminists are viewed as subversive when they "dare" to take on traditionally male practices. While the women might articulate that the practices are deeply meaningful to them, their audience instead ascribes it to a political motive rather than personal spirituality. This type of misread symbol is also present in LGBTQ pride symbols, which are often unrecognizable to those outside of the community. Moreover, those that are recognized can still be misinterpreted, as was the case with the rainbow Star of David flag at the Chicago Dyke March. The flag represented a celebration of overlapping Jewish and lesbian identity for the women carrying it, but it was interpreted as a sign of Zionism and as anti-Palestinian by parade organizers, who ultimately used it to exclude and silence the women at the march.

The pink triangle also articulates an overlapping identity or, at least, a shared history. The use of this symbol is perceived differently by Holocaust survivors (and even members of the Jewish community) than it is by young adults, especially those who have tattooed it on their body without full recognition of the history the symbol holds. This difference in perception drives the tension of the symbol: is the pink triangle a symbol that can be reappropriated in positive ways despite its horrific history?

In other instances, the multiplicity of symbolic meaning is less publicly overt. For example, in the thick description of feminist *upsherin* in chapter 3, the mothers describe experiencing a tension that they were having "fake" *upsherin* for their daughters unlike the "real" *upsherin* they might have had for their sons. Similarly, *upsherin* has traditionally been viewed as an Orthodox practice, but the women hosting feminist *upsherin* see their feminist ritual as a quintessentially un-Orthodox practice. The symbol of the first haircut in the Orthodox understanding demonstrates a shift from mother to father's care for the boy; the first haircut of the feminist *upsherin* represents the ongoing role of the parent and a larger community of women in raising young Jewish girls.

Third, the examples given in the previous chapters articulate a reconceptualization of the gendered Jewish body. This is done in two primary ways: by inventing practice and by reinterpreting practice. The feminist *upsherin* described in chapter 3 is a clear example of inventive ritual. These rituals also include the other innovative feminist practices described in chapter 3 like *Rosh Chodesh* celebrations or the *mikveh* ceremony for African American and Jewish women cleansing themselves of racism. By entering the *mikveh* with their bodies, the women take a personal belief or experience (i.e., combatting racism or addressing the personal wounds of racism) and literally embody their convictions and experiences. In these ways, gender is fore fronted as part of the body; that is to say, the corporeal experience of the woman is centered in meaningful ways that demonstrate how the body interacts with belief. Whether it is the feminist *upsherin* or a new *mikveh* ceremony, the female body is prioritized in the ritual, highlighting the ways in which women and feminists have created religious and spiritual meaning by developing their own body rituals.

Other feminist body rituals have been developed as analogous alternatives to traditionally male rituals (e.g., the *bat mitzvah)*; that does not lessen the importance of these rituals. Indeed, in their reconceptualization of the Jewish body, they broaden what is considered an "acceptable" body. This includes adaptive rituals like *pidyon ha-bat* or *simchat bat*, as well as practices that have been incorporated from other faith traditions like yoga or meditation breath sounds. These latter practices, popular in the Renewal movement, demonstrate how utilizing a variety of practices can help create inclusive environments for all Jews. By broadening the traditional understanding of how bodies are presented or encountered in Jewish spaces, there is an acknowledgment that there is not one right way to be a Jew or to conceptualize the Jewish body.

Finally, the examples offered in the previous chapters highlight the body as a space for the transmission of culture and community formation. This can be seen in how feminist bodies in the synagogue challenge cultural norms and create space for the next generation of Jewish women. The same is true of feminist *upsherin*, where women create communities of support and of spiritual engagement for both the mother and the daughter. Moreover, these communities of women commit to educating and raising empowered girls— lessons that include both how to navigate Jewishness as a woman and how to navigate being a woman Jewishly.

Other communities also find their foothold around shared symbols, including the LGBTQ young adult application of the pink triangle as a way of establishing a shared legacy and history for queer communities. This is reflected, also, in LGBTQ Jewish pride symbols, which challenge the lack of social scripts, helping individuals learn how to exist as a Jew in queer spaces and as a member of the LGBTQ community in Jewish spaces.

In the end, the framework laid out in this book articulates a commitment to feminist theory that is coupled with folkloristics, specifically the folklore of the body. The examples given in these chapters highlight the potential multiplicity of applications of feminist bodylore within Judaism, as they articulate how symbols are used as a space for identity communication in deep and meaningful ways. Yet, this is not an exhaustive treatment of Jewish feminist bodylore. In fact, it is only the beginning.

So, why does any of this matter? I would like to suggest five potential ways that Jewish feminist bodylore could be applied going forward: by highlighting the experiences of the transgender community, by addressing the whitewashing of Jewish bodies, by describing age, by discussing digital space, and by considering the lives of differently abled Jews.

Feminist theory has not always been attentive to the needs of the transgender community. As I have written these chapters, I have been very aware of the gender binaries that much of traditional feminist discourse has employed. Now, as feminist methodologies work to debunk gender binaries (while still attending to the voices of women when they are otherwise silenced), the experiences of the transgender, nonbinary, and gender nonconforming communities also need to be centered. Jewish feminist bodylore offers the tools for discussing inventive ritual, celebrations of the Jewish trans identified body, and a platform for discussions of embodiment in a system that is predicated on binaries. To be a truly feminist methodological application, Jewish feminist bodylore cannot function at the expense of trans bodies, but must, instead, consider how the nonbinary or trans body can be conceptualized Jewishly, investigating what rituals are being invented or adapted to meet the religious and spiritual needs of trans Jews.

In line with the erasure of trans narratives in much of Jewish analysis, there has been a generalized whitewashing of the Jewish body. It bears repeating: not all Jews are white. The lives of Jews of Color should be foregrounded in meaningful ways that speak to the nuance and complexities of existing in a world where both Jews and non-Jews say things like, "You don't look Jewish!" Jewish feminist bodylore offers the tools to unpack questions about the body narrative of what makes a body look Jewish and how bodies feel and are experienced by Jewish to Jews of Color.

Another overlooked part of how the Jewish body is scripted is age. In the previous chapters I have discussed childhood rituals for girls, but there exist other inventive rituals that mark age or life transitions. Judaism has familiar coming of age rituals (e.g., the *bat mitzvah*, confirmation, or the wedding), but there are also other rituals that mark childbirth, divorce, the end of menses, physical aging, and death that engage the body in deeply spiritual ways.

Previous discussions of Jewish LGBTQ culture have hinted at the role of the digital body or digital space in shaping conceptualizations of the body. As identified earlier in this conclusion, the privatization of the social sphere is now also driven by the ability to exist as virtual bodies. This begs the question, how are Jewish bodies scripted in digital culture and, at the same time, how does one learn Jewish culture through digital forms? In particular, when looking at marginalized Jewish voice (e.g., Jews of Color, disabled Jews, LGBTQ Jews), how do they utilize digital spaces to foster community and challenge the status quo?

Finally, crucial to body studies is the understanding that bodies are differently abled. As demonstrated in chapter 2's treatment of women's bodies in the Renewal movement, the circle can be expanded to include Jews of all abilities. This discussion necessitates, at a minimum, consideration of both the experience of the individual and the imposed limitations of the space. In other words, Jewish feminist bodylore can aid in unpacking the ways in which differently abled bodies are scripted in Judaism, but at the same time it is critical to apply these same methodologies to consideration of how Jewish spaces preclude the full integration of all bodies into the congregation. Space dictates whether or not individuals have full access and experiences of religious life. Even the best of intentions can still fall short if there is not fully accessible space, which goes beyond simply adhering to building accessibility codes. Jewish feminist bodylore offers the tools to explore questions about how differently abled bodies can be celebrated Jewishly and how the bodies of differently abled Jews encounter themselves in Jewish spaces.

Feminist bodylore is able to evolve alongside of the bodies it investigates, allowing for overlapping identities and for an expansive treatment of the body. It offers the tools to consider the multifaceted ways in which bodies can be engaged—whether that be within an ethno-religious group like Judaism or within other groups. In the end, our bodies, which are so often overlooked in other analysis, are the canvas of the self, where we engage and embody that which is important to us alongside that which intrinsically constitutes our selfhood and identity. At the same time, others interpret our bodies as text, whether they understand our symbols or even see our own bodies in the same way that we do. The tensions caused by misperceptions highlight the marginality of both the Jewish and the feminist body, that they are not fully recognized even within their own communities—and this lack of recognition is especially poignant when Jewishness, feminism, and/or queerness overlap and operate together.

Recently I hosted a workshop for a Jewish Sisterhood. The women asked me to speak about the ways that the Sisterhood could support Jewish women's literal physical bodies. I prepared a discussion of the incorporation of women's bodies in synagogue life, examples of how spaces could be pro-breastfeeding, affirming of a Jewish women's right to chose whether or not she wanted to be pregnant, and body positive for young Jewish girls; additionally, I also prepared a few challenges about how the Sisterhood could work to be inclusive of queer and trans identified bodies. Falling back on the student-centered learning techniques I use in my own college classroom, at the beginning of the workshop I asked the women to draw examples of Jewish bodies, both how they see them and how they are stereotyped. As we went around the room and shared our sketches, we reached four-year-old Lexy, who was sitting next to her mother. We had all mistakenly assumed she was coloring in her coloring book, but she volunteered her own picture of a Jewish body. She held up a piece of paper that had a heart with a large toothy grin, two googly eyeballs, a small nose, spindly arms and legs, and a series of small yellow beams of light radiating around the heart. As Lexy explained, you can't actually draw a Jew because you only know a Jew by her heart. I clasped my hands together, turned to the women, and said, "My work here is done. This generation has got it figured out!" May we all learn to be a little bit more like Lexy, to embrace the many manifestations of personhood on the body, to celebrate them, and to recognize that there is no one right or wrong way to embody Jewishness.

NOTES

1. Some scholars and activists have used the phrase post-feminism to refer to those who continue to embody the spirit of second and third wave feminism but push back against the whiteness of classical feminism, as well as the gender binaries that traditional feminism has utilized. But this is not the sense in which I hear common colloquial usage of the phrase.

Glossary

Adonai   [Hebrew] Lit. My Lord; one of the names used to refer to God. *Adonai* appears in the Hebrew Bible as one of the names for God and is also one of the acceptable substitutions for speaking the name of God when reading the *tetragrammaton*.

Ashkenazic Jews   Lit. from the region of Germany and northern France called "Ashkenaz" during the Middle Ages; refers to Jews with German and Eastern European roots.

Alef-bet   [Hebrew] The first two letters of the Hebrew alphabet, used to refer to the entire alphabet; a Jewish learning ritual, often paired with *upsherin*, in which a child reads the Hebrew alphabet aloud for the first time as part of a larger ritual commemorating community support of the child's education.

Aliya   [Hebrew] Lit. to rise up or ascend; when an individual is called to the *bimah* to recite a blessing before and after the Torah reading.

Amidah   [Hebrew] A central Jewish prayer; also referred to as "the Standing Prayer" or the *Shmoneh Esreh.*

Atarah   [Hebrew] Lit. the crown; refers to the collar of the *tallis*.

B'not Kohen   [Hebrew] Daughters of a *Kohen*, a specific designation within Judaism that references (traditionally patrilineal) descent from Aaron.

Bar Mitzvah (pl. B'nai Mitzvah)   [Hebrew] A Jewish coming of age ritual for boys at the age of 13.

Bat Mitzvah (pl. B'not Mitzvah)   [Hebrew] A Jewish coming of age ritual for girls at the age of 12 or 13; also referred to in Yiddish as *Bas Mitzvah* (pl. *B'nos Mitzvah*).

Bimah   [Hebrew] The platform area in the synagogue; the place from where scripture is read.

Bochur   [Hebrew/Yiddish] A young unmarried Jewish man, usually referring to a yeshiva student; sometimes also spelled *bokhur*.

Brit bat   [Hebrew] A Jewish naming ceremony for newborn girls; an analogous ritual created for a *brit milah*; also sometimes referred to as *simchat bat*.

Brit milah   [Hebrew] A Jewish religious male circumcision ceremony performed on the eighth day of the boy's life; also referred to in Yiddish as a *bris*.

Caftan   [Arabic] A robe or tunic worn over the clothes.

Cantor   [Latin] A Jewish clergy person trained and ordained to lead the congregation in prayer; also sometimes referred to as the *hazzan*.

Challah (pl. challot)   [Hebrew] A Jewish bread that is braided and eaten on the Sabbath and most Jewish holidays; in order to be *halakhic*, challah is made from dough which has had a small portion set aside as an offering.

Dastaar   [Punjabi] A religious turban worn as part of Sikhism that is mandatory for all initiated Sikh men and women.

Daven   [Yiddish] to pray; this sometimes is used colloquially to refer to ecstatic prayer, typified by rocking and bowing, although it refers generally to all prayer.

Davening   [Yiddish/English] an Anglicization of the Yiddish *daven* to create an active verb meaning to be in prayer or to pray.

Ervah   [Hebrew] Lit. nakedness; referring to things which traditionally have been considered sexually erotic or arousing.

Golellet   [Hebrew] The roller of the Torah who replaces the cover after it is read.

Halakha   [Hebrew] The collective body of Jewish law; can also reference individual Jewish laws.

Halakhic   [Hebrew] Pertaining to Jewish legal codes or Jewish law; in accordance with *halakha*.

Hamentashen   [Yiddish] Lit. Haman pockets; the triangular-shaped filled cookies that are associated with Purim.

Hamsa   [Arabic/Hebrew] A palm or hand shaped amulet with an eye pictured in the middle; also known as the Hand of Fatima; believed to provide defense against the evil eye.

HaShem   [Hebrew] Lit. The Name; a way of referencing the name of God; one of the acceptable spoken substitutions for the *tetragrammaton*.

Havurah (pl. havurot)   [Hebrew] Lit. fellowship; a small group, pairing, or community of like-minded Jews who learn and worship together.

Hazzan   [Hebrew] A Jewish clergy person trained and ordained to lead the congregation in prayer; also referred to as the *cantor*.

Hijab   [Arabic] The veil or head covering worn by some Muslim women when they are in the presence of men outside of their immediate family; the hijab covers the head and the chest.

Horah   [Greek/Bulgarian] A type of circle dance; in Jewish contexts the *horah* is often danced to the folk tune *Hava Nagila* and features prominently at Jewish life cycle events and weddings.

Kabbalah   [Hebrew] Lit. the received tradition; an esoteric school of mystical thought that works to understand the relationships between the eternal and the mortal.

Karan   [Hebrew] To send forth beams; a Latin mistranslation of a description of Moses replaced *karan* with *keren* (a horn) and yielded the stereotype of Jews having horns.

Keren   [Hebrew] A horn; a Latin mistranslation of a description of Moses replaced *karan* (to send forth beams) with *keren* and yielded the stereotype of Jews having horns.

Kiddush   [Hebrew] The blessing said over wine during the Sabbath and Jewish holidays.

Kiddushin   [Hebrew] The sanctification or dedication during a wedding in which the two partners are believed to be in holy union.

Kippah (pl. kippot)   [Hebrew] Cap, the traditionally male Jewish skullcap now also worn by women; the Anglicized plural is sometimes rendered kippahs; also known as *yarmulke* in Yiddish.

Kippah sruga   [Hebrew] Referring to the types of *kippot* worn by Religious Zionists; referring to the knitted or crocheted kippah.

Kittel   [Yiddish] From the German for housecoat; a white robe that is worn, typically by men or clergy, on special occasions including the High Holy Days or by Ashkenazic men at their weddings; the kittel is also used as part of traditional male burial adornment.

Klal Yisrael   [Hebrew] The collective responsibility for the Jewish community.

Kol isha   [Hebrew] The voice of a woman; within Orthodox Judaism, men are traditionally not allowed to hear women sing as the female voice is considered *ervah* (naked or sexually arousing).

Kotel   [Aramaic] The Western Wall, also known as the Wailing Wall, in Jerusalem. Believed to be part of Second Jewish Temple, connected to the Temple Mount, which holds religious significance for Christians, Jews, and Muslims.

Labrys   [Greek] A double-bitted or double-bladed axe.

Magbiaha   [Hebrew] The individual who ritually lifts the Torah.

Maharat   [Hebrew] An acronym for *Morah Hilchatit Ruchanut Toranit*, which means "Torah-based, spiritual teacher, according to Jewish law"; used as a title by Orthodox female clergy as an alternative to rabbi or rabba.

Mechitza (pl. mechitzot)   [Hebrew] A partition that separates men and women in the sanctuary of the synagogue.

Megillah Esther [Hebrew] The Book of Esther; often shortened to Megillah when referring to reading the book of Esther during the celebration of Purim.

Menorah [Hebrew] A seven-lamp lamp-stand or candelabra that is a symbol for Judaism; colloquially used to refer to a *hanukkiah*, which is the nine-branched candelabrum used during Hanukkah.

Mezuzah (pl. mezuzot) [Hebrew] A box or decorative case that houses a piece of parchment containing the Hebrew verses Deuteronomy 6:4-9 and 11:13-21; these are hung on the doorposts and doorways of Jewish homes.

Midrash (pl. midrashim) [Hebrew] Traditionally rabbinic literature that contains interpretations and commentaries on the Torah, Talmud, and other Jewish texts and *halakha*; contemporary Midrash includes any interpretation of Jewish texts and beliefs and especially aims to resolve problems or tensions created by difficult texts or principles.

Mikveh (pl. mikvot) [Hebrew] The bath used for ritual immersion; the ritual bath used to remove or nullify ritual impurities.

Minyan (pl. minyanim) [Hebrew] Traditionally the quorum of ten men required for certain religious events and rituals; contemporary egalitarian understandings of this practice expand it to include ten men or women.

Mitzvah (pl. mitzvot) [Hebrew] A commandment, understood to be of divine origin.

Nerot [Hebrew] The lighting of candles, especially on the Sabbath or on holidays; typically a *mitzvah* ascribed to women.

Niddah [Hebrew] A woman who is considered ritually impure during the time of menstruation; pertaining to the laws of family or sexual purity.

Niggun (pl. niggunim) [Hebrew] A tune or melody sung as part of Jewish liturgy or practice; often characterized by repetitive sounds (i.e., lai-lai-lai or bim-bim-bam) instead of lyrics.

Payot [Hebrew] Sidelocks or sidecurls worn by Jewish men; also known as *payos* in Yiddish.

Pidyon ha-ben [Hebrew] The ritual that commemorates the redemption of the first-born son in which five silver coins are given to a *Kohen*.

Pidyon ha-bat [Hebrew] The ritual that commemorates the redemption of the first-born daughter in which five silver coins are given to a *Kohen;* created as an analogous ritual to the *pidyon ha-ben.*

Rabbi [Latin/Greek] A teacher of Torah; an ordained leader and clergyperson within Judaism.

Rebbe [Yiddish] Refers to the *rabbi* but also to a teacher or mentor who is not ordained; used within Hasidic practice to refer to the leader of each Hasidic movement.

Rosh Chodesh [Hebrew] The new Jewish month; begins with the appearance of the new moon; associated with women's gatherings.

Seder [Hebrew] Lit. order or arrangement; the Jewish ritual feast that marks the beginning of Passover.

Sephardic Jews [Hebrew] Jews with Spanish and north-African roots.

Shabbat [Hebrew] The Jewish Sabbath; also known as *Shabbos* in Yiddish.

Shabbos [Yiddish] The Jewish Sabbath; also known as *Shabbat* in Hebrew.

Shaddai [Hebrew] One of the names of God used by Jews.

Shema [Hebrew] also referred to as the *Shema Yisrael* (lit. Hear, O Israel); the centerpiece of and most important Jewish prayer that affirms the monotheistic oneness of God

Shofar [Hebrew] A ram's horn that is sounded like a bugle as part of Jewish practice, including during Rosh Hashanah, Yom Kippur, and on weekday mornings in the month of Elul.

Shtreimel (pl. shtreimlech) [Yiddish] Fur hats worn by Hasidic men; the plural is often Anglicized to *shtreimels*.

Shuckling [Yiddish] Lit. to shake; refers to the swaying, rocking, or bowing during Jewish prayer; sometimes also spelled *shokeling*.

Siddur (pl. Siddurim) [Hebrew] A Jewish prayer book, including the set order of daily prayers, Sabbath service, and other Jewish services.

Simchat Bat [Hebrew] A Jewish naming ceremony for newborn girls; an analogous ritual created for a *brit milah*; also sometimes referred to as *brit bat*.

Tallis (pl. tallisim) [Yiddish] The prayer shawl worn over the shoulders or head; the plural is often Anglicized to *tallises*.

Tallit (pl. tallitot) [Hebrew] The prayer shawl worn over the shoulders or head; the plural is often colloquially shortened to *tallit*.

Talmud [Hebrew] Lit. instruction or teaching; a central Jewish text that deals with religious laws and textual interpretation.

Tefillin [Hebrew] The leather cases enclosing scripture written on parchment that are bound to the forehead and left arm; also known as *phylacteries* from the Greek.

Tekhinos (pl. tekhinot) [Yiddish] Personal prayers or supplications written in the vernacular; historically especially common among women who could not read or write in the liturgical language; sometime also spelled *tkhines*.

Tetragrammaton [Greek] Lit. "[consisting of] four letters"; refers to the four-letter name for God given in the Bible. Jews traditionally do not pronounce this name nor do they read aloud transliterated forms of the name (e.g., Yahweh); instead, the name is substituted with alternatives like *Adonai* or *HaShem*.

Torah [Hebrew] Lit. instruction, teaching, law; the first five books of the Hebrew Bible; traditionally read from a handwritten scroll.

Tzedakah   [Hebrew] Lit. justice or righteousness; used to refer to charity as an ethical obligation and not a spontaneous act of generosity; a mandatory religious obligation performed regardless of one's personal socioeconomic standing.

Tzitzit   [Hebrew] The knotted ritual fringes worn by Jews.

Upsherin   [Yiddish] Lit. to shear off; a haircutting ceremony for Jewish children, typically for Orthodox boys at the age of three; often performed in tandem with the *alef-bet* ritual; sometimes also spelled *opsherin* or *up-sherinish*.

Yarmulke (pl. yarmulkes)   [Yiddish] The traditionally male Jewish skull-cap now also worn by women; also known as *kippah* in Hebrew.

Yeshiva (pl. yeshivot)   [Hebrew/Yiddish] A Jewish educational institution or school that focuses on the daily study of traditional religious texts, particularly the Talmud and Torah.

Bibliography

Abes, Elisa S. 2011. "Exploring the Relationship between Sexual Orientation and Religious Identities for Jewish Lesbian College Students." *Journal of Lesbian Studies* 15(2): 205–25.

Adelman, Penina Villenchik. 1990. *Miriam's Well: Rituals for Jewish Women Around the Year*. New York: Holmes and Meier.

Adler, Rachel. 1972. "The Jew Who Wasn't There: Halacha and the Jewish Woman." *Off Our Backs* 2(6): 16–17.

Alexander, Elizabeth Shanks. 2011. "Women's Exemption from Shema and Tefillin and How These Rituals Came to be Viewed as Torah Study." *Journal for the Study of Judaism* 42(4–5): 531–79.

Ali, Shainna, and Sejal Barden. 2015. "Considering the Cycle of Coming Out: Sexual Minority Identity Development." *The Professional Counselor* 5(4): 501–15.

Alpert, Rebecca. 1998. *Like Bread on a Seder Plate: Jewish Lesbians and the Transformation of Tradition*. New York: Columbia University Press.

Alpert, Rebecca, Sue Levi Elwell, and Shirley Idelson. 2001. *Lesbian Rabbis: The First Generation*. New Jersey: Rutgers University Press.

Amit, Aaron. 2008. "The Curious Case of Tefillin: A Study in Ritual Blessings." *Jewish Studies Quarterly* 15(4): 268–88.

Anti Defamation League. 2017. "ADL To Urban Outfitters: Remove Tapestry 'Eerily Reminiscent' of Holocaust Garb." https://www.adl.org/news/press-releases/adl-to-urban-outfitters-remove-tapestry-eerily-reminiscent-of-holocaust-garb.

Antony, Mary Grace. 2014. "It's Not Religious, but It's Spiritual: Appropriation and the Universal Spirituality of Yoga." *Journal of Communication and Religion* 37(4): 63–81.

Ariel, Yaakov. 2007. "Gay, Orthodox, and Trembling: The Rise of Jewish Orthodox Gay Consciousness, 1970s–2000s." *Journal of Homosexuality* 52(3–4): 91–109.

Askew, Kelly M. 1998. Ambiguous Discourses; Performative Approaches to Gender and Race. *American Anthropologist* 100(4): 1030–33.

Avishai, Orit. 2008. "Doing Religion in a Secular World: Women in Conservative Religions and the Question of Agency." *Gender and Society* 22(4): 409–33.

Avodah Dance. n.d. "Mission." http://www.avodahdance.org.

Babcock, Barbara. 1987. "Taking Liberties, Writing from the Margins, and Doing It with a Difference." *Journal of American Folklore* 100(389): 390–411.

Baizerman, Suzanne. 1992. "The Jewish *kippah sruga* and the Social Construction of Gender in Israel." In *Dress and Gender: Making and Meaning,* edited by Ruth Barnes and Joanne B. Eicher, 92–105. New York: Berg Publishers.

Balka, Christie, and Andy Rose. 1991. *Twice Blessed: On Being Lesbian, Gay, and Jewish.* Boston: Beacon Press.

Barrow, Katie M., and Katherine A. Kuvalanka. 2011. "To be Jewish and Lesbian: An Exploration of Religion, Sexual Identity, and Familial Relationships." *Journal of GLBT Family Studies* 7(1): 470–92.

Bartky, Sandra Lee. 1990. *Femininity and Domination: Studies in the Phenomenology of Oppression,* New York: Routledge.

Bascom, William. 1954. "Four Functions of Folklore." *Journal of American Folklore* 67: 333–49.

Baskin, Judith R. 2001. "Women and Ritual Immersion in Medieval Ashkenaz: The Sexual Politics of Piety." In *Judaism in Practice: From the Middle Ages Through the Early Modern Period,* edited by Lawrence Fine, 131–42. New Jersey: Princeton University Press.

Batza, Katie. 2018. *Before AIDS: Gay Health Politics in the 1970s.* Philadelphia: University of Pennsylvania Press.

Beaton, Mary Elizabeth, and Hannah B. Washington. 2015. "Slurs and the Indexical Field: The Pejoration and Reclaiming of Favelado 'Slum-dweller.'" *Language Sciences* 52: 12–21.

Ben-Amos, Dan. 1976. *In Praise of Baal Shem Tov (Shivhei Ha-Besht: The Earliest Collection of Legends About the Founder of Hasidism).* New York: Jason Aronson, Inc.

Bendix, Regina. 2000. "The Pleasures of the Ear: Toward an Ethnography of Listening." *Cultural Analysis* 1(2000): 33–55.

Berenbaum, Michael, ed. 1990. *A Mosaic of Victims: Non-Jews Persecuted and Murdered by Nazis.* New York: New York University Press.

Berkowitz, Leah. 2009. "This is What a Rabbi Looks Like: Buy a T-Shirt." https://thisiswhatarabbilookslike.wordpress.com/buy-a-shirt/.

Berrin, Susan, ed. 1998. *Celebrating the New Moon: A Rosh Chodesh Anthology.* New York: Jason Aronson, Inc.

Beusterien, John L. 1999. "Jewish Male Menstruation in Seventeenth-Century Spain." *Bulletin of the History of Medicine* 73(3): 447–56.

Bianchi, Claudia. 2014. "Slurs and Appropriation: an Echoic Account." *Journal of Pragmatics* 66: 35–44.

Bilge, Sirma. 2010. "Beyond Subordination vs. Resistance: An Intersectional Approach to the Agency of Veiled Muslim Women." *Journal of Intercultural Studies* 31(1): 9–28.

Birke, Lynda. 2000. *Feminism and the Biological Body*. New Brunswick, NJ: Rutgers University Press.

Blackstock, Claire Maria Chambers. 2008. "The Rhetoric of Ritual: Transformation as Revelation and Congregational Liturgical Dance as Performance Theory." *Performance Research* 13(3): 100–108.

Blau, Yoram. 2003. "From Milah (Circumcision) to Milah (Word): Male Identity and Rituals of Childhood in the Jewish Ultraorthodox Community." *Ethos*. 31(2): 172–203.

Bleir, Ruth. 1984. *Science and Gender: A Critique of Biology and its Theories on Women*. New York: Pergamon.

Bloomfield, Diane. 2004. *Torah Yoga: Experiencing Jewish Wisdom through Classical Postures*. New York: John Wiley and Sons.

Booker, Janice L. 1991. *The Jewish American Princess and Other Myths: The Many Faces of Self-hatred*. New York: Shapolsky Publishers.

Bornstein, Kate. 1994. *Gender Outlaw: On Men, Women, and the Rest of Us*. New York: Routledge.

Boyarin, Daniel. 1997. *Unheroic Conduct: The Rise of Heterosexuality and The Invention of the Jewish Man*. Berkley: University of California Press.

Boyarin, Daniel, Daniel Itzkovitz, and Ann Pelligrini. 2003. *Queer Theory and the Jewish Question*. New York: Columbia University Press.

Brettschneider, Marla. 2003. "Ritual Encounters of the Queer Kind: A Political Analysis of Jewish Lesbian Ritual Innovation." *Journal of Lesbian Studies* 7(2): 29–48.

Brodkin, Karen. 1998. *How Jews Became White Folks and What That Says about Race in America*. New Jersey: Rutgers University Press.

Broner, Esther M. 1999. *Bringing Home the Light: A Jewish Woman's Handbook of Rituals*. New York: Council Oaks.

Bronner, Leila Leah. 1993. "From Veil to Wig: Jewish Women's Hair Covering." *Judaism: A Quarterly Journal of Jewish Life and Thought* Fall: 465–77.

Bronner, Simon J. 2005. *Manly Traditions: The Folk Roots of American Masculinities*. Indiana: Indiana University Press.

———. 1982. "The Haptic Experience of Culture." *Anthropos* 77(3/4): 351–62.

———. 2010. "Framing Folklore: An Introduction." *Western Folklore* 69(3/4): 275–97.

Brown, Angela. 2004. *Mentsh: On Being Jewish and Queer*. Los Angeles: Alyson Books.

Budgeon, Shelley. 2015. "Theorizing Subjectivity and Feminine Embodiment: Feminist Approaches and Debates." *Handbook of Children and Youth Studies*: 243–56.

Burke, Kelsy C. 2012. "Women's Agency in Gender-Traditional Religions: A Review of Four Approaches." *Sociology Compass* 6(2): 122–33.

Butler, Judith. 1990. *Gender Trouble: Feminism and the Subversion of Identity*. New York: Routledge.

———. 1993. *Bodies that Matter: On the Discursive Limits of Sex*. London: Routledge.

———. 2004. *Undoing Gender*. New York: Routledge.

Carrell, Barbara Goldman. 1999. "Hasidic Women's Head Coverings." In *Religion, Dress and the Body*, edited by Linda B. Arthur, 163–80. Oxford, UK: Oxford University Press.

CCAR. 2015. "Resolution on the 25th Anniversary of the Report of the Ad Hoc Committee on Homosexuality and the Rabbinate and the Acceptance of Openly Gay and Lesbian Rabbinic Students at HUC-JIR." https://www.ccarnet.org/ccar-resolutions/acceptance-openly-gay-and-lesbian-rabbinic-student/.

Chamberlain, A. F. 1893. "Human Physiogonomy and Physical Characteristics in Folk-Lore and Folk-Speech." *The Journal of American Folklore* 6(20): 13–24.

Chauncey, George. 2009. *Why Marriage: The History Shaping Today's Debate Over Gay Equality*. New York: Basic Books.

Charmé, Stuart Z. 2014. "When Yoga Is Kosher but Kabbalah Is Not: Spirituality and Cultural Appropriation in Jewish Education." *Religion and Education* 41(3): 273–89.

Cheek, Cheryl, and Kathleen W. Piercy. 2004. "Quilting as Age Identity Expression in Traditional Women." *The International Journal of Aging and Human Development* 59(4): 321–37.

Cho, Sumi, Kimberlé Williams, and Leslie McCall. 2013. "Toward a Field of Intersectional Studies: Theory, Application, and Praxis." *Signs: Journal of Women in Culture and Society* 38(4): 785–810.

Clair, Leonard L., and Alan B. Govenar. 1981. *Stoney Knows How: Life as a Tattoo Artist: Tattooing Since 1928*. Knoxville: University Press of Kentucky.

Classen, Constance. 2012. *The Deepest Sense: A Cultural History of Touch*. Chicago: University of Illinois Press.

Cohen, Baruch Joseph. 1950. "The Structure of the Synagogue Prayer-Chant." *Journal of the American Musicological Society* 3(1): 17–32.

Cohen, Debra Nussbaum. 2008. "Jewish Renewal: An Introduction to the Jewish Renewal Movement." https://www.myjewishlearning.com/article/jewish-renewal/.

Cohen, Judah M. 2009. *The Making of the Reform Jewish Cantor: Musical Authority, Cultural Investment*. Bloomington: Indiana University Press.

Cohen, Steven Martin. 1980. American Jewish Feminism: A Study in Conflicts and Compromises. *American Behavioral Scientist* 23(4): 519–58.

Cohen, Steven M., Caryn Aviv, and Ari Kelman. 2009. "Gay, Jewish, or Both?" *Journal of Jewish Communal Service* 84(1–2): 154–66.

Cohn, Yehuda. 2008. *Tangled Up in Text: Tefillin and the Ancient World*. Providence, RI: Brown Judaic Studies.

Cooey, Paula M., William R. Eakin, and John B. McDaniel. 1991. *After Patriarchy: Feminist Transformations of the World Religions*. London: Sri Satguru Publications.

Cooper, Alanna E. 2014. "A Little Girl's First Haircut." *Lilith*. http://lilith.org/articles/a-little-girls-first-haircut/.

Croom, Adam M. 2014. "The Semantics of Slurs: A Refutation of Pure Expressivism." *Language Sciences* 41: 227–42.

CU Boulder Libraries. 2014. "Embodied Judaism: The Sound of Ecstasy." https://www.youtube.com/watch?v=D6ThOS49ZmV.

Darwin, Helana. 2017. "Jewish Women's Kippot: Meanings and Motives." *Contemporary Jewry* 37(1): 81-97.

———. 2018. "Redoing Gender, Redoing Religion." *Gender and Society* 32(3): 348–70.

Davis, Eli, and Elise Davis. 1983. *Hats and Caps of the Jews*. Jerusalem: Masada.

Davis, Kathy. 1997. *Embodied Practices*, London: Sage.

———. 2008. "Intersectionality as Buzzword: A Sociology of Science Perspective on What Makes a Feminist Theory Successful." *Feminist Theory* 9(1): 67–85.

De Beauvoir, Simone. 1953. *The Second Sex*. London: Jonathan Cape.

De Lange, Naydene, Claudia Mitchell, Lebo Moletsane, Jean Stuart, and Thabisile Buthelezi. 2006. "Seeing with the Body: Educators Representations of HIV and AIDS." *Journal of Education* 38(1): 45–66.

Diprose, Rosalyn. 1994. *The Bodies of Women: Ethics, Embodiment and Sexual Difference*. London: Routledge.

Dorson, Richard. 1972. "Introduction: Concepts of Folklore and Folklife Studies." In *Folklore and Folklife: An Introduction*, edited by Richard M. Dorson, 1–50. Chicago: University of Chicago Press.

Drinkwater, Gregg. 2016. "Judaism and Sexuality." *The Wiley Blackwell Encyclopedia of Gender and Sexuality Studies*. New Jersey: Wiley Blackwell.

Duberman, Martin Baumel. 1990. "Twice Blessed or Doubly Other?" *Tikkun* 5(2): 102–5.

Dubrofsky, Rachel E. 2013. "Jewishness, Whiteness, and Blackness on Glee; Singing to the Tune of Post-Racism." *Communication, Culture, and Critique* 6(1): 82–102.

Dundes, Alan. 1964. "On Game Morphology: A Study of the Structure of Non-Verbal Folklore." *New York Folklore* 20(4): 276.

Dunlap, Andy. 2014. "Coming-out Narratives Across Generations." *Journal of Gay and Lesbian Social Services* 26(3): 318–35.

Edelman, S.M. 2000. "To Pass or Not to Pass, That is the Question: Jewish Cultural Identity in the United States." In *AmongUS: Essays on Identity, Belonging, and Intercultural Competence*, edited by Myron W. Lustig and Jolene Koester, 33–40. New York: Allyn and Bacon.

Edelstein, Monika D. 2002. "Lost Tribes and Coffee Ceremonies: Zar Spirit Possession and the Ethno-Religious Identity of Ethiopian Jews in Israel." *Journal of Refugee Studies* 15(2): 153–70.

Ehrlich, Howard J. 1962. "Stereotyping and Negro-Jewish Stereotypes." *Social Forces* 41(2): 171–76.

Ehrlich, Uri. 2004. *The Nonverbal Language of Prayer: A New Approach to Jewish Liturgy*. Germany: Mohr Siebeck.

Ehrman, Yisroel. 2000. *Tefillin: Making the Connection: A User-Friendly Guide to the Laws and Significance of Tefillin*. New York: Feldheim Publishers.

Elman, R. Amy. 1996. "Triangles and Tribulations: the Politics of Nazi Symbols." *Journal of Homosexuality* 30(3): 1–11.

Elper, Ora Wiskind. 2003. *Traditions and Celebrations of the Bat Mitzvah*. New York: Urim.

Farrer, Claire R. 1975. *Women and Folklore*. Austin: University of Texas Press.

Farrow, John T., and J. Russell Herbert. 1982. "Breath Suspension During the Transcendental Meditation Technique." *Psychosomatic Medicine* 44(2): 133–53.

Faulkner, Sandra L., and Michael L. Hecht. 2010. "The Negotiation of Closetable Identities: A Narrative Analysis of Lesbian, Gay, Bisexual, Transgendered Queer Jewish Identity." *Journal of Social and Personal Relationships* 28: 829–47.

Feldman, Walter Z. 1994. "Bulgărească/Bulgarish/Bulga: The Transformation of a Klezmer Dance Genre." *Ethnomusicology* 38(1): 1–35.

Ferber, Abby L. 1999. *White Man Falling: Race, Gender, and White Supremacy*. New Jersey: Rowman and Littlefield.

Fine, David J. 2002. "Women and the Minyan: Committee on Jewish Law and Standards of the Rabbinical Assembly." https://www.rabbinicalassembly.org/sites/default/files/public/halakhah/teshuvot/19912000/oh_55_1_2002.pdf.

Firestone, Shulamith. 1970. *The Dialectic of Sex: the Case for Feminist Revolution*. London: The Women's Press.

Fishman, Sylvia Barack. 1995. *A Breath of Life: Feminism and the American Jewish Community*. Waltham, MA: Brandeis University Press.

Foxman, Abraham H. 2010. *Jews and Money: The Story of a Stereotype*. New York: St. Martin's Press.

France, David. 2017. *How to Survive a Plague: The Story of How Activists and Scientists Tamed AIDS*. New York: Vintage.

Frankiel, Tamar, and Judy Greenfield. 1997. *Minding the Temple of the Soul: Balancing Body, Mind, and Spirit through Traditional Jewish Prayer, Movement, and Meditation*. Philadelphia: Jewish Lights Publishing.

Gatens, Moira, 1996. *Imaginary Bodies: Ethics, Power and Corporeality*. London and New York: Routledge.

Gechter, Elisha. 2015. "My Daughter Asked for an Upsherin." *JOFA's Torch*, https://www.myjewishlearning.com/the-torch/my-daughter-asked-for-an-upsherin/.

Geertz, Clifford. 1973. "Thick Description: Toward an Interpretive Theory of Culture." In *The Interpretation of Cultures: Selected Essays*, by Clifford Geertz, 3–30. New York: Basic Books.

Gershom, Yonassan. n.d. "Story of Reb Zalman's B'nai Or Tallit." https://havurahshirhadash.org/story-of-reb-zalmans-bnai-or-tallit/.

Gilman, Sander L. 1986. *Jewish Self-Hatred: Anti-Semitism and the Hidden Language of the Jews*. Baltimore: Johns Hopkins University Press.

———. 1990. "The Jewish Body: A "Footnote." *Bulletin of the History of Medicine* 64(4): 588–602.

———. 1991. *The Jew's Body*. New York: Routledge.

———. 1994. "Or, the History of the Nose Job." In *The Other in Jewish Thought and History: Constructions of Jewish Culture and Identity*, edited by Lawrence J. Silberstein and Robert L. Cohn, 364. New York: NYU Press.

Gloster, Rob. 2017. "Iconic San Francisco Synagogue is No Longer 'Just' for LGBT Jews." *The Times of Israel*. https://www.timesofisrael.com/iconic-san-francisco-synagogue-is-no-longer-just-for-lgbt-jews/.

Goffman, Erving. 1959. *The Presentation of Self in Everyday Life*. New York: Anchor.

———. 1961. *Asylums: Essays on the Social Situation of Mental Patients and Other Inmates*. New York: Routledge.

———. 1965. Identity Kits. In *Dress, Adornment and the Social Orders*, edited by M. Roach and J. Eicher, 246–47. New York: John Wiley and Sons.

———. 1974. *Frame Analysis: An Essay on the Organization of Experience*. New York: Harper and Row.

Goldberg, Harvey E. 1987. "Torah and Children: Symbolic Aspects of the Reproduction of Jews and Judaism." In *Judaism Viewed from Within and from Without: Anthropological Studies*, edited by Harvey E. Goldberg, 107–31. Albany: State University of New York Press.

Goldberg, Silke Muter. 2005. Language and Gender in Early Modern and 19th Century Jewish Devotional Literature. *Gender, Tradition, and Renewal*, edited by Robert L. Platzner, 93. Chicago: Peter Lang.

Goldstein, Eric L. 2006. *The Price of Whiteness: Jews, Race, and American Identity*. New Jersey: Princeton University Press.

Gould, Deborah B. 2009. *Moving Politics: Emotion and ACT UP's Fight Against AIDS*. Chicago: University of Chicago Press.

Grau, Günter, and Claudia Shoppman, eds. 2013. *The Hidden Holocaust?: Gay and Lesbian Persecution in Germany, 1933–45*. New York: Routledge.

Greenberg, Simon, ed. 1988. *The Ordination of Women as Rabbis: Studies and Response*. New York: The Jewish Theological Seminary of America.

Greenberg, Steven. 2004. *Wrestling with God and Men: Homosexuality in the Jewish Tradition*. Madison: University of Wisconsin Press.

Greene, Virginia. 1992. "Accessories of Holiness: Defining Jewish Sacred Objects." *Journal of the American Institute for Conservation* 31(1): 31–39.

Groesberg, Sholom. 2008. *Jewish Renewal: A Journey: The Movement's History, Ideology, and Future*. New York: iUniverse, inc.

Gross, Rita M. 1996. *Feminism and Religion: An Introduction*. Boston: Beacon Press.

Grossman, Susan, and Rivka Haut. 1992. *Daughters of the King Women and the Synagogue: A Survey of History, Halakhah, and Contemporary Realities*. Philadelphia: Jewish Publication Society.

Grosz, Elizabeth. 1994. *Volatile Bodies: Toward a Corporeal Feminism*. Bloomington: Indiana University Press.

Guest, Deryn. 2006. *The Queer Bible Commentary*. New York: Scm-Canterbury Press.

Haeberle, Erwin J. 1981. "Swastika, Pink Triangle, and Yellow Star: The Destruction of Sexology and the Persecution of Homosexuals in Nazi Germany." *The Journal of Sex Research* 17(3): 270–87.

Halbertal, Tova Hartman, and Irit Koren. 2006. *Between "Being" and "Doing": Conflict and Coherence in the Identity Formation of Gay and Lesbian Orthodox Jews*. New York: American Psychological Association.

Harrison-Kahan, Lori. 2005. "Passing for White, Passing for Jewish: Mixed Race Identity in Danzy Senna and Rebecca Walker." *Melus* 30(1): 19–48.

Hazon. n.d. "Elat Chayyim: Renewing Jewish Spiritual Practices for Sustaining Futures." https://www.hazon.org/isabella-freedman/elat-chayyim/.

Heger, Heinz. 1970. *Die Männer mit dem Rosa Winkel.* Berlin: Merlin Verlag.

Heinz, Bettina, et al. 2002. "Under the Rainbow Flag: Webbing Global Gay Identities." *International Journal of Sexuality and Gender Studies* 7(2–3): 107–24.

Helmreich, William B. 1982. *The Things They Say Behind Your Back: Stereotypes and the Myths Behind Them.* New York: Transaction Publishers.

Heschel, Susannah. 1987. *On Being a Jewish Feminist.* New York: Schocken.

———. 1991. "Jewish Feminism and Women's Identity." *Women and Therapy* 10(4): 31–39.

Heskes, Irene. n.d. "Cantors: American Jewish Women." https://jwa.org/encyclopedia/article/cantors-american-jewish-women.

Hillel International. 2018. "I'm Jewish and Queer." https://www.facebook.com/HillelFJCL/photos/a.135810598330.109451.77273593330/10156383363503331/?type=3&theater.

Hodges, Frederick Mansfield. 2001. "The Ideal Prepuce in Ancient Greece and Rome: Male Genital Aesthetics and Their Relation to Lipodermos, Circumcision, Foreskin Restoration, and the Kynodesme." *Bulletin of the History of Medicine* 75(3): 375–405.

Holden, Harold Miller. 1950. *Noses.* New York: World Publishing Company.

Hollis, Susan Tower, Linda Pershing, and M. Jane Young. 1993. *Feminist Theory and the Study of Folklore.* Urbana: University of Illinois Press.

Hunter, Susan. 2006. *AIDS in America.* New York: St. Martin's Press.

Hurtado, Aida. 1996. *The Color of Privilege: Three Blasphemies on Race and Feminism.* Ann Arbor: University of Michigan Press.

Huss, Boaz. 2007. "The New Age of Kabbalah: Contemporary Kabbalah, the New Age, and Postmodern Spirituality." *Journal of Modern Jewish Studies* 6(2): 107–25.

Hyman, Paula E. 1995. *Gender and Assimilation in Modern Jewish History: The Roles and Representations of Women.* Seattle: University of Washington Press.

Idel, Moshe. 2012. *Hasidism: Between Ecstasy and Magic.* New York: SUNY Press.

Ingber, Judith Brin. 2011. *Seeing Israeli and Jewish Dance.* Detroit, MI: Wayne State University Press.

Institute for Contemporary Midrash. n.d. "Torah Alive! Community Based Trainings." http://www.icmidrash.org/community-based-trainings-residencies/.

Irby, Courtney A. 2014. "Dating in Light of Christ: Young Evangelicals Negotiating Gender in the Context of Religious and Secular American Culture." *Sociology of Religion* 75(2): 260–83.

Itzhaky, Haya, and Karni Kissil. 2015. "It's A Horrible Sin. If They Find Out, I Will Not Be Able to Stay: Orthodox Jewish Gay Men's Experiences of Living in Secrecy." *Journal of Homosexuality* 62(5): 621–43.

Jacobs, Joseph. 1886. "On the Racial Characteristics of Modern Jews." *The Journal of the Anthropological Institute of Great Britain and Ireland* 15: 23–62.

———. 1906. "Nose" in *Jewish Encyclopedia*, edited by Maurice Fishberg. New York: Funk and Wagnalls.

Jacobs, Louis. 1972. *Hasidic Prayer*. New York: Taylor and Francis.

Jacobson, Matthew Frye. 1999. *Whiteness of a Different Color*. Boston: Harvard University Press.

Jakobsen, Janet R. 2003. "Queers are Like Jews, Aren't They? Analogy and Alliance Politics." In *Queer Theory and the Jewish Question*, edited by Daniel Boyarin, Daniel Itzkovitz, and Anne Pelligrini, 64–89. New York: Columbia University Press.

Jay, Karla, and Allen Young. 1978. *Lavender Culture: The Perceptive Voices of Outspoken Lesbians and Gay Men*. New York: New York University Press.

Jensen, Erik N. 2002. "The Pink Triangle and Political Consciousness: Gays, Lesbians, and the Memory of Nazi Persecution." *Journal of the History of Sexuality* 11(1) 310–49.

Jones, Amelia, and Andrew Stephensen. 2005. *Performing the Body/Performing the Text*. New York: Routledge.

Jones, Cleve. 2017. *When We Rise: My Life in the Movement*. New York: Hachette Books.

Johnston, Ruth D. 2006. "Joke-Work: The Construction of Jewish Postmodern Identity in Contemporary Theory and American Film." In *You Should See Yourself: Jewish Identity in Postmodern American Culture*, edited by Vincent Brook, 207-29. New Brunswick, NJ: Rutgers University Press.

Jordan, Rosan, and Susan Kalcik. 1985. *Women's Folklore, Women's Culture*. Philadelphia: University of Pennsylvania Press.

Jorgensen, Jeana. 2008. "Innocent Initiations: Female Agency in Eroticized Fairy Tales." *Marvels and Tales* 22(1): 27–37.

Kaczorowski, Craig. 2013. "Paragraph 175." *GLBTQ: An Encyclopedia of Gay, Lesbian, Bisexual, Transgender, and Queer Culture*. http://www.glbtqarchive.com/ssh/paragraph_175_S.pdf.

Kahn, Yoel H. 1989. "Judaism and Homosexuality: The Traditionalist/Progressive Debate." *Journal of Homosexuality* 18(3/4): 47–82.

Kapchan, Debora. 1996. *Gender on the Market: The Revoicing of Tradition in Beni Mellal, Morocco*. Philadelphia: University of Pennsylvania Press.

Kaplan, Aryeh. 1985. *Jewish Meditation: A Practical Guide*. New York: Random House.

Katz, David S. 1999. "Shylock's Gender: Jewish Male Menstruation in Early Modern England." *The Review of English Studies* 50(200): 440–62.

Katz, Jonathan Ned. 1989. "Signs of the Times: The Making of Liberation Logos." *The Advocate* October 10: 29.

Keshet. n.d. "Our Story." https://www.keshetonline.org/about/our-story.

Kimmel, Michael. 2009. *Guyland: The Perilous World Where Boys Become Men*. New York: Harper Perennial.

Kisliuk, Michelle. 1997. "(Un)doing Fieldwork: Sharing Songs, Sharing Lives." In *Shadows in the Field: New Perspectives for Fieldwork in Ethnomusicology*, edited by Gregory Bartz and Timothy Cooley, 23–44. New York: Oxford University Press.

Klapheck, Elisa, and Toby Axelrod. 2004. *Fräulein Rabbiner Jonas: The Story of the First Woman Rabbi*. New York: Jossey-Bass Inc.

Klepfisz, Irena. 1989. "Secular Jewish Identity: Yidishkayt in America." In *The Tribe of Dina: A Jewish Women's Anthology*, edited by Melanie Kantrowitz and Irena Klepfisz, 32–50. Boston: Beacon Press.

Klug, Brian. 2003. "The Collective Jew: Israel and the New Antisemitism." *Patterns of Prejudice* 37(2): 117–38.

Konner, Melvin. 2009. *The Jewish Body*. New York: Schocken.

Kousaleos, Nicole. 1999. "Feminist Theory and Folklore." *Folklore Forum* 3(1/2): 19–34.

Krawitz, Cole. 2004. "A Voice from Within: A Challenge for the Conservative Jewish Movement and its Gay/Lesbian Activists." *Nashim: A Journal of Jewish Women's Studies and Gender Issues* 8(1): 165–74.

Kroha, Lucienne. 2014. *The Drama of the Assimilated Jew: Giorgio Bassani's Romanzo di Ferrara.* Toronto: University of Toronto Press.

Langmuir, Gavin I. 1990. *History, Religion, and Antisemitism.* Oakland: University of California Press.

Laqueur, Walter. 2006. *The Changing Face of Anti-Semitism: From Ancient Times to Present Day*. London: Oxford University Press.

Lautmann, Rüdiger. 1981. "The Pink Triangle: The Persecution of Homosexual Males in Concentration Camps in Nazi Germany." *Journal of Homosexuality* 6(1/2): 141–60.

Leighton, Cora E. 2012. "Real Girl Dance in Mummer Throng: A Performative Historiography of Gender in the Philadelphia Mummers Parade." *Text and Performance Quarterly* 32(January): 38–58.

Levitt, Laura. 1997. *Jews and Feminism: An Ambivalent Search for Home*. New York: Psychology Press.

Lewis, Mary Ellen B. 1974. "The Feminists Have Done It: Applied Folklore." *The Journal of American Folklore* 87(343): 85–87.

LGBTs & FRIENDS Against the Misuse of the Pink Triangle. n.d. "About This Group." https://www.facebook.com/groups/lgbtsagainstmisuseofpinktriangle/about.

Luther, Martin. 1543/1948. *On the Jews and Their Lies*. London: Gottfried and Fritz.

Magid, Shaul. 2013. *American Post-Judaism: Identity and Renewal in a Postethnic Society.* Bloomington: Indiana University Press.

Malkin, Yaakov. 2004. *Secular Judaism: Faith, Values, and Spirituality.* New York: Vallentine Mitchell.

Mannes, Stefan. 1999. *Antisemitismus im nationalsozialistischen Propagandafilm: Jud Süss und Der ewige Jude*. Berlin: Teiresias-Verlag.

Marcus, Eric. 1992. *Making History: The Struggle for Gay and Lesbian Equal Rights, 1945–1990: An Oral History.* New York: Harper Collins.

Mark, Elizabeth Wyner. 2003. *The Covenant of Circumcision: New Perspectives on an Ancient Jewish Rite.* Waltham, MA: Brandeis University Press.

Mark, Naomi. 2008. "Identities in Conflict: Forging an Orthodox Gay Identity." *Journal of Gay and Lesbian Mental Health* 12(3): 179–194.

Marshall, Stuart. 1991. "The Contemporary Political Use of Gay History: The Third Reich," in *How Do I Look? Queer Film and Video,* edited by Bad Object Choices, 65–102. Seattle: Bad Object Choices.

Martin, Emily. 1987. *The Woman in the Body: A Cultural Analysis of Reproduction.* Milton Keynes: Open University Press.

McCall, Richard D. 2007. *Do This: Liturgy as Performance.* Notre Dame, IN: University of Notre Dame Press.

McLeer, Anne. 1998. "Saving the Victim: Recuperating the Language of the Victim and Reassessing Global Feminism." *Hypatia* 13(1): 41–55.

Mechling, Jay. 2008. "Paddling and Repressing of the Feminine in Male Hazing." *Boyhood Studies* 2(1): 60–75.

Merwin, Ted. 2007. "Jew-Face: Non-Jews Playing Jews on the American Stage." *Cultural and Social History* 4(2): 215–33.

Mill, John Stuart, and Harriet Taylor Mill. 1970. *Essays on Sex Equality*: Chicago: University of Chicago Press.

Miller, Shane Aaron. 2010. Making Boys Cry: The Performative Dimensions of Fluid Gender. *Text and Performance Quarterly* 30(April): 162–82.

Milligan, Amy K. 2013. "Colors of the Jewish Rainbow: A Study of Homosexual Jewish Men and Yarmulkes." *Journal of Modern Jewish Studies* 12(1): 71–89.

———. 2014a. *Hair, Headwear, and Orthodox Jewish Women: Kallah's Choice.* Lanham, MD: Lexington Books.

———. 2014b. "Expanding Sisterhood: Jewish Lesbians and Externalizations of Yiddishkeit." *Journal of Lesbian Studies* 18(4): 437–55.

———. 2017. "Hair Today, Gone Tomorrow: Upsherin, Alef-Bet, and the Childhood Navigation of Jewish Gender Identity Symbol Sets." *Children's Folklore Review* 38(1): 7–25.

———. 2018. "Bodylore and Dress." In *The Oxford Handbook of American Folklore and Folklife Studies,* edited by Simon J. Bronner. New York: Oxford University Press.

Mills, Margaret. 1993. "Feminist Theory and the Study of Folklore: A Twenty-Year Trajectory Toward Theory." *Western Folklore* 52(1): 157–92.

Mohanty, Chandra Talpade. 2003. *Feminism Without Borders: Decolonizing Theory, Practicing Solidarity.* New York: Zubaan.

Montagu, Ashley. 1971. *Touching: The Human Significance of the Skin.* New York: Columbia University Press.

Nadell, Pamela. 1998. *Women Who Would Be Rabbis: A History of Women's Ordination 1889–1985.* Boston: Beacon Press.

Narayan, Uma, ed. 2000. *Decentering the Center: Philosophy for a Multicultural, Postcolonial, and Feminist World.* Bloomington: Indiana University Press.

Ner-David, Haviva. 2000. *Life on the Fringes: A Feminist Journey Toward Traditional Rabbinic Ordination.* Needham: JFL Books.

Niculescu, Mira. 2012. "I the Jew. I the Buddhist." *CrossCurrents* 62(3): 350–59.

Novick, Leah. 2014. *On the Wings of Shekhinah: Rediscovering Judaism's Divine Feminine.* New York: Quest Books.

Novick, Peter. 2000. *The Holocaust and Collective Memory: The American Experience.* London: Bloomsbury.

Nyhagen, Line, and Beatrice Halsaa. 2016. *Religion, Gender, and Citizenship: Women of Faith, Gender Equality, and Feminism.* London: Springer.

O'Brien, Mary. 1981. *The Politics of Reproduction.* London: Routledge and Kegan Paul.

Ochs, Vanessa. 2010. *Inventing Jewish Ritual.* Philadelphia: Jewish Publication Society.

Ophir, Natan. 2014. *Rabbi Shlomo Carlebach: Life, Mission, and Legacy.* New York: Urim Publications.

Paredes, Américo, and Richard Bauman. 1972. *Toward New Perspectives in Folklore.* Austin: University of Texas Press.

Parkins, Wendy. 2000. "Protesting Like a Girl: Embodiment, Dissent, and Feminist Agency." *Feminist Theory* 1(1): 59–78.

Pelligrini, Ann. 1997. *Performance Anxieties: Staging Psychoanalysis, Staging Race.* New York: Routledge.

Personal Narratives Group, eds. 1989. *Interpreting Women's Lives: Feminist Theory and Personal Narratives.* Bloomington: Indiana University Press.

Pink, Sarah. 2015. *Doing Sensory Ethnography.* New York: Sage.

Pinson, DovBer. 2010. *Upsherin: Exploring the Laws, Customs, and Meanings of a Boy's First Haircut.* New York: Iyyun Center for Jewish Spirituality.

Pitts-Taylor, Victoria. 2015. "A Feminist Carnal Sociology? Embodiment in Sociology, Feminism, and Naturalized Philosophy." *Qualitative Sociology* 38(1): 19–25.

Plant, Richard. 2011. *The Pink Triangle: The Nazi War Against Homosexuals.* New York: Holt Paperbacks.

Plaskow, Judith. 1991. *Standing Again at Sinai: Judaism from a Feminist Perspective.* San Francisco: Harper and Row.

———. 1997. "Jewish Feminist Thought." In *History of Jewish Philosophy*, edited by Daniel H. Frank and Oliver Leaman, 885–95. New York: Routledge.

Plaskow, Judith, and Carol P. Christ. 1989. *Weaving the Visions: New Patterns in Feminist Spirituality.* San Francisco: Harper and Row.

Plaskow, Judith, and David Shneer. 2009. *Torah Queeries: Weekly Commentaries on the Hebrew Bible.* New York: NYU Press.

Polen, Nehemia. 1992. "Miriam's Dance: Radical Egalitarianism in Hasidic Thought." *Modern Judaism* 12(1): 1–21.

Ponse, Barbara. 1978. *Identities in the Lesbian World: The Social Construction of Self.* Westport, CT: Greenwood Press.

Poole, Ross. 2010. "Misremembering the Holocaust: Universal Symbol, Nationalist Icon, or Moral Kitsch?" In *Memory and the Future*, edited by Yifat Gutman, Adam D. Brown, and Amy Sodaro, 31–49. London: Palgrave Macmillan.

Prell, Riv-Ellen. 1989. *Prayer and Community: The Havurah in American Judaism.* Indiana: Wayne State University Press.

———. 1999. *Fighting to Become American: Jews, Gender, and the Anxiety of Assimilation.* Boston: Beacon Press.

Preminger, Beth. 2001. "'The Jewish Nose' and Plastic Surgery: Origins and Implications." *Journal of the American Medical Association* 286(17): 21–61.

Price, Janet, and Margrit Shildrick. 2017. *Feminist Theory and the Body: A Reader.* New York: Routledge.

Propp, William H. 1987. "The Skin of Moses' Face: Transfigured or Disfigured?" *The Catholic Biblical Quarterly* 49(3): 375–86.

Prown, Jules David. 1982. "Mind in Matter: An Introduction to Material Culture Theory and Method." *Winterthur Portfolio* 17(1): 1–19.

Radler, Joan. 1993. *Feminist Messages: Coding Women's Folk Culture.* Illinois: University of Illinois Press.

Radner, Joan N., and Susan S. Lanser. 1987. "The Feminist Voice: Strategies of Coding in Folklore and Literature." *The Journal of American Folklore* 100(398): 412–25.

Rao, Aliya H. 2015. "Gender and Cultivating the Moral Self in Islam: Muslim Converts in an American Mosque." *Sociology of Religion* 76(4): 413–35.

Rapoport, Chaim. 2004. *Judaism and Homosexuality: An Authentic Orthodox View.* London: Vallentine Mitchell.

Reimer, Joseph. 2007. "Beyond More Jews Doing Jewish: Clarifying the Goals of Informal Jewish Education." *Journal of Jewish Education* 73(1): 5–23.

Reilly, Andrew, and Eirik J. Saethre. 2013. "The Hankie Code Revisited: From Function to Fashion." *Critical Studies in Men's Fashion* 1(1): 69–78.

Reisigl, Martin, and Ruth Wodak. 2005. *Discourse and Discrimination: Rhetorics of Racism and Antisemitism.* New York: Routledge.

Resnick, Irven M. 2000. "Medieval Roots of the Myth of Jewish Male Menses." *Harvard Theological Review* 93(3): 241–63.

Rethelyi, Mari. 2014. "Hungarian Nationalism and the Origins of Neolog Judaism." *Nova Religion: The Journal of Alternative and emergent Religions* 18(2): 67–82.

Reznik, David. 2010. *I Usually Know a Jew When I See One?: Race, American Jewish Identity, and 21st Century US Film.* Gainesville: University of Florida Press.

Rich, Adrienne, 1979. *Of Women Born, Motherhood as Experience and Institution,* London, Virago.

———. 1986. "Split at the Root: An Essay on Jewish Identity." In *Adrienne Rich's Poetry and Prose,* 224–38. New York: W.W. Norton.

Robinson, Olivia F., and C.F. Robinson. 1995. *The Criminal Law of Ancient Rome.* London: Duckworth.

Rosario, Margaret, Eric W. Schrimshaw, and Joyce Hunter. 2008. "Predicting Different Patterns of Sexual Identity Development Over Time Among Lesbian, Gay, and Bisexual Youths: A Cluster Analytic Approach." *American Journal of Community Psychology* 42(3–4): 266–82.

Rose, H.A. 1919. "The Language of Gesture." *Folklore* 30(4): 312–15.

Rosenberg, Larry. 2004. *Breath by Breath: The Liberating Practice of Insight Meditation.* New York: Shambhala Publications.

Ross, Sarah M. 2016. *A Season of Singing: Creating Feminist Jewish Music in the United States.* Waltham, MA: Brandeis University Press.

Rothenberg, Celia E. 2006a. "New Age Jews: Jewish Shamanism and Jewish Yoga." *Jewish Culture and History* 8(3): 1–21.

———. 2006b. "Jewish Yoga: Experiencing Flexible, Sacred, and Jewish Bodies." *Nova Religio: The Journal of Alternative and Emergent Religions* 10(2): 57–74.

Rothenberg, Celia E., and Anne Vallely. 2008. *New Age Judaism*. New York: Vallentine Mitchell.

Rowe, Karen E. 1999. "To Spin a Yarn: The Female Voice in Folklore and Fairy Tale." In *Women as Storytellers*, edited by Maria Tartar, 297–308. New York: Norton.

Ruah-Midbar, Marianna. 2012. "Current Jewish Spiritualties in Israel: A New Age." *Modern Judaism* 32(1): 102–24.

Ruddick, Sara. 1989. *Maternal Thinking: Towards a Politics of Peace*. New York: Ballantine Books.

Ruther, Rosemary Radford. 1998. *Religion and Sexism: Images of Women in the Jewish and Christian Traditions*. New York: Wipf and Stock Publishers.

Ruttenberg, Danya. 2001. *Yentl's Revenge: The Next Wave of Jewish Feminism*. New York: Seal Press.

Saposnik, Irv. 1994. "Jolson, the Jazz Singer, and the Jewish Mother: Or how my Yiddishe Momme became my Mammy." *Judaism* 43(4): 432.

Schachter-Shalomi, Zalman, and Joel Segel. 2012. *Davening: A Guide to Meaningful Jewish Prayer*. Philadelphia: Jewish Lights Publishing.

Schilts, Randy. 2007. *And the Band Played On: Politics, People, and the AIDS Epidemic*. New York: St. Martin's Griffin.

Schimel, Lawrence. 2002. *Found Tribe: Jewish Coming Out Stories*. New York: Sherman Asher Publishing.

Schliefer, Eliyahu. 1995. "Current Trends of Liturgical Music in the Ashkenazi Synagogue." *The World of Music* 37(1): 59–72.

Schnoor, Randal F. 2006. "Being Gay and Jewish: Negotiating Intersecting Identities." *Sociology of Religion* 67(1): 43–60.

Schoppmann, Claudia. 1996. *Days of Masquerade: Life Stories of Lesbians During the Third Reich*. New York: Columbia University Press.

Schrank, Bernice. 2007. "Cutting Off Your Nose to Spite Your Race: Jewish Stereotypes, Media Images, Cultural Hybridity." *Shofar: An Interdisciplinary Journal of Jewish Studies* 25(4): 18–42.

Schreiber, Lynne. 2006. *Hide and Seek: Jewish Women and Hair Covering*. New York: Urim Publications.

Sennett, Richard. 1977. *The Fall of Public Man*. New York: WW Norton & Company.

Shneer, David, and Caryn Aviv. 2002. *Queer Jews*. New York: Rutledge.

Shokeid, Moshe. 1995. *A Gay Synagogue in New York*. New York: Columbia University Press.

Shuman, Amy. 1993. "Gender and Genre." In *Feminist Theory and the Study of Folklore*, edited by Susan Tower Hollis, Linda Pershing, and M. Jane Young, 71–85. Urbana: University of Illinois Press.

Sieczkowski, Cavan. 2017. "Urban Outfitters Under Fire for Selling Tapestry Reminiscent of Uniforms Worn by Gay Nazi Prisoners." https://www.huffingtonpost.com/2015/02/10/urban-outfitters-tapestry-gay-prisoner-uniforms_n_6652934.html.

Sifakis, Carl. 2005. *The Mafia Encyclopedia*. New York: Facts on File.

Silbiger, Steve. 2000. *The Jewish Phenomenon: Seven Keys to the Enduring Wealth of a People*. New York: Longstreet Press.

Singer, Ellen. 1993. *Paradigm Shift: From the Jewish Renewal Teachings of Reb Zalman Schachter-Shalomi*. New York: Jason Aronson.

Silverman, Eric. 2012. *A Cultural History of Jewish Dress*. Oxford: Berg.

Sklar, Deidre. 1994. "Can Bodylore be Brought to Its Senses?" *Journal of American Folklore* 107(423): 9–22.

Smallwood, E. Mary. 2001. *The Jews Under Roman Rule: From Pompey to Diocletian: A Study in Political Relations*. London: Leiden.

Solomon, Daniel J. 2017. "How Rabbis are Trying to Make the Conservative Movement More Gay Friendly." https://forward.com/news/371280/how-rabbis-are-trying-to-make-the-conservative-movement-more-gay-friendly/.

Stanton, Elizabeth Cady, Susan B. Anthony, and Matilda Joslyn Gage. 1887. *History of Women's Suffrage*. New York: Anthony Rochester.

STI Video Transcripts. 1997. Box 9. Institute of Contemporary Midrash Records. Post-Holocaust American Judaism Collection, University of Colorado-Boulder.

Stoeltje, Beverly J. 1988. "Gender Representation in Performance: The Cowgirl and the Hostess." *Journal of Folklore Research* 25(3): 219–41.

Stratton, Jon. 2001. "Not Really White-Again: Performing Jewish Difference in Hollywood Films Since the 1980s." *Screen* 42(2): 142–66.

Straus, Raphael. 1942. "The Jewish Hat as an Aspect of Social History." *Jewish Social Studies* 4(1): 59–72.

Stryker, Susan, and Jim Van Buskirk. 1996. *Gay by the Bay: A History of Queer Culture in the San Francisco Bay Area*. New York: Chronicle Books.

Svigals, Alicia. 1998. "Why We Do This Anyway: Klezmer as Jewish Youth Subculture." *Judaism* 47(1): 43.

Sztokman, Elana Maryles. 2011. *The Men's Section: Orthodox Jewish Men in an Egalitarian World*. Waltham, MA: Brandeis University Press.

Tabb Stewart, David. 2017. "LGBT/Queer Hermeneutics and the Hebrew Bible." *Currents in Biblical Research* 15(3): 289–314.

Taylor, Archer. 1956. "The Shanghai Gesture." *FF Communications*: 166.

Tedlock, Dennis. 1990. "From Voice and Ear to Hand and Eye." *Journal of American Folklore* 103(408): 133–56.

Truth, Sojourner. 1851. "Ain't I A Woman?" Ain't I A Woman. http://www.feminist.com/resources/artspeech/genwom/sojour.htm.

Turner, Victor, and Edith Turner. 1982. "Performing Ethnography." *Drama Review* 26: 33–50.

Umansky, Ellen M. 2005. *From Christian Science to Jewish Science: Spiritual Healing and American Jews*. New York: Oxford University Press.

Walton, Rivka M. 2011. "Lilith's Daughters, Miriam's Chorus: Two Decades of Feminist Midrash." *Religion & Literature* 43(2): 115–27.

Weininger, Otto. 1932. *Geschlect und Charakter: Eine Prinzipielle Untersuchung*. Berlin: G. Kiepenheuer.

Weisberg, Dvorah E. 1992. "On Wearing Tallit and Tefillin." In *Daughters of the King Women and the Synagogue: A Survey of History, Halakhah, and Contemporary Realities,* 282–84. Philadelphia: Jewish Publication Society.

Weiss, Bari. 2017. "I'm Glad the Dyke March Banned Jewish Stars." *New York Times* Opinion. https://www.nytimes.com/2017/06/27/opinion/im-glad-the-dyke-march -banned-jewish-stars.html.

Weiss, Gail. 2013. *Body Images: Embodiment as Intercorporeality*. New York: Routledge.

Weiss-Rosmarin, Trude. 1970. "The Unfreedom of Jewish Women." *Jewish Spectator* 35: 2–7.

Weissler, Chava. 2006. "Women of Vision in the Jewish Renewal Movement: The Eschet Hazon [Woman of Vision] Ceremony." *Jewish Culture and History* 8(3): 62-86.

———. 2007. "art is spirituality!: practice, play, and experiential learning in the jewish renewal movement." *Material Religion* 3(3): 354–79.

———. 2010. *Art as Spiritual Practice in the Jewish Renewal Movement*. Ann Arbor: University of Michigan Press.

West, Candace, and Don H. Zimmerman. 1987. "Doing Gender." *Gender and Society* 1(2): 125–51.

Whisnant, Clayton J. 2016. *Queer Identities and Politics in Germany: A History, 1880-1945.* New York: Columbia University Press.

Winland, Daphne Naomi. 1993. "The Quest for Mennonite Peoplehood: Ethno-Religious Identity and the Dilemma of Definitions." *Canadian Review of Sociology* 30(1): 110–38.

Witz, Anne. 2000. "Whose Body Matters? Feminist Sociology and the Corporeal Turn in Sociology and Feminism." *Body and Society* 6(2): 1–24.

Wollstonecraft, Mary. 1996. *A Vindication of the Rights of Woman.* Mineola, NY: Dover Publications.

Yingling, Thomas E. 1997. *AIDS and the National Body*. Durham, NC: Duke University Press.

Yocom, Margaret. 1985. "Woman to Woman: Fieldwork and the Private Sphere." In *Women's Folklore, Women's Culture*, edited by Rosan Jordan and Susan Kalcik, 45–53. Philadelphia: University of Pennsylvania Press.

Yoder, Don. 1972. "Folk Costume." In *Folklore and Folklife: An Introduction*, 295–323. Chicago: University of Chicago Press.

Young, Katharine. 1993. *Bodylore*. Knoxville: University of Tennessee Press.

———. 1994. "Whose Body? An Introduction to Bodylore." *Journal of American Folklore* 107(423): 3–8.

———. 2011. "Gestures, Intercorporeity, and the Fate of Phenomenology in Folklore." *Journal of American Folklore* 124(492): 55–87.

Young, Iris Marion. 2005. *On Female Body Experience: "Throwing Like a Girl" and Other Essays*. New York: Oxford University Press.

Zimmerman, Bonnie, ed. 1999. "Symbols." *Encyclopedia of Lesbian and Gay Histories and Cultures*, edited by George Haggerty and Bonnie Zimmerman, 747. Abingdon, UK: Routledge.

Index

About the Author

Amy K. Milligan is the Batten Endowed Assistant Professor of Jewish Studies and Women's Studies at Old Dominion University, where she is also the director of the Institute of Jewish Studies and Interfaith Understanding. She is the author of *Hair, Headwear, and Orthodox Jewish Women: Kallah's Choice* (Lexington, 2014), as well as numerous journal articles on Jewish embodiment. As an ethnographer, she explores the folkloric manifestations of selfhood and identity on the body and uses these questions of bodylore to consider lived experiences of gender, sexuality, and Jewishness. Her work also probes the experiences of small or marginalized Jewish communities.

Lightning Source UK Ltd.
Milton Keynes UK
UKHW021314290721
387981UK00016B/312